A Case for Beauty

History and Philosophy of Code Enforcement

Eugene Alper

Cover illustration: *Evagrius Ponticus as a Hermit*
by Johann Sadeler (Rijksmuseum, Amsterdam)
Cover design: MGI Studio

To Warren Campbell, Ph.D. for his guidance and inspiration

To Maria Gracia Inglessis, Ph.D. for her guidance, inspiration,
and everything else

CONTENTS

ACKNOWLEDGEMENT

This book about code enforcement is an accident. If the author were, for example, a better actor, the book might be about the craft of acting. If he were a better linguist, it might be about languages or translations. But as it happened, he spent a number of years enforcing municipal codes (a strange activity too, almost as strange as making funny faces or playing with foreign words). And at some point, without him asking, random thoughts, questions, and answers about code enforcement started coming to his mind. More accurately, they started coming *through* his mind. And because he knew they were not his—they were merely passing through him, as if sent by someone on their way to somewhere—he thought his duty was to pay respect to the little transients. He thought that to honor them was to try to give them material existence, that is, to express them in language, as best as he could. Without being materialized in speech or chiseled on a tablet or printed on a page, he thought, who would ever know about them? Hence the physical object you are holding is an imperfect catch of some beautiful creatures that have once swum through the author's net. But while the book's subject may be an accident, the fact of its writing is not. For no matter where we are, no matter what occupation we happen to pursue, at some point we all start wondering about its meaning. This book, while it happens to be about code enforcement, is the materialization of this common-to-all search.

To my colleagues with whom at different times and under different circumstances I have shared the joys and burdens of code enforcement, and to others who knew more than me and generously shared their knowledge—Vyto Adomaitis, Jeff Aubel, Gloria Aviles, Steve Bailey, Eric Barela, Tom Benedetti, Yessica Benitez, Warren Campbell, Jason Cosylion, Jim Donovan, Edward Espinoza, Manuel Gallegos, Jeff Jones, Tony Leyva, Elisa Lopez, Dan Mick, Brent Mullins, Yellena Orloff, Danny Rivas, Rex Shields, Jeff Skorneck, Dan Smith, Jeff Strong, Melissa Tin, Andy Torres, and Joe Torres—thank you.

1
WHY READ THIS BOOK?

This book is a historical analysis of a government function known as code enforcement.

Wait. This is a sure way to lose your reader right from the start. Why would anyone care to read *a historical analysis* of *a government function*? Who cares about government functions at all, especially from long ago?

The answer is that you may want to read about government functions because they are projections of what takes place in your own heart. Governments—with their boring manuals and procedures, with their hard-nosed inspectors carrying clipboards and checking off boxes—they would not be there if you, my esteemed reader, did not have irrepressible wishes and desires in your heart. If your heart did not swing, sometimes violently, between freedom and order; if it did not seek a balance between the two; if it did not yearn for beauty as freedom and order's peaceful reconciliation, the colorless bureaucracies and dull administrators would not be there. So, if you are interested in what takes place in your own heart (and I have yet to find anyone who isn't) you may want to see what the heart has wrought. You may want to read about government functions. You may want to know one of them, code enforcement, because looking at this tiny sliver of government functions, you will see a microscopic image projected on a large screen, and you will glimpse into the minute operations of your heart.

What is code enforcement anyway? As a municipal job, it began as a younger cousin to building, fire, and health inspection, and it grew in the last several decades into a mature adult. It took over some duties that had been historically performed by its older relatives, but it acquired new ones as well. Simply by being there, as it always happens when someone takes their job seriously, code enforcement has stimulated new areas of regulation; it has enlarged and deepened its own field. Today, code enforcement regulates noise, housing, business licensing, land use, historical preservation, short-term rentals, signage, animals, mobile billboards, environmental protection, to name just a few. Because of its expansion, code enforcement is often the only unit that has the holistic view of the entire municipal code and knows how to enforce it. Because of its broad reach, code enforcement has grown in importance and become a handy tool of problem solving and developed into a profession distinct from others. But its birth and expansion, as I will argue throughout the book, is significant for more serious reason. Code enforcement allows us to detect the pulse of civilization itself. It is not so much the old duties that code enforcement took over from others that will interest us, but the new ones. Observing that code enforcement does today what was not done a hundred years ago indicates, in my opinion, to an interesting phase in Western history. It is not a wholly new phase, to be sure; human nature is unchangeable, and it is impossible for anything fundamentally new to happen in human affairs; history repeats itself with only slight variations. The interesting phase I am referring to is simply a resurgence of a familiar pattern. From basic to sophisticated, from earthly to lofty, from licentious to orderly, from orderly to beautiful, and then crashing again into basic and earthly—this pulsating pattern of civilization is what I believe we can detect in the birth and growth of code enforcement.

The questions I am asking in this book are, What social function does code enforcement perform? Why was it not needed before and why is it needed now? The answers, I suggest, are found as we look in the mirror. The permanent feature of our nature and a recurring pattern in history, is that as soon as we secure basic safety and functionality of our environment, we begin beautifying it. Code enforcement's nascent signs can be found as early as in Colonial America, but its beautification phase takes place in the modern city. In early history, code enforcement's role was to secure the basic needs of the human body. In today's affluent cities, its role is often to enforce urban beauty enshrined into law. Hence the title of the book.

2
DOES CODE ENFORCEMENT EXIST?

In government, the professions are the conveyor belts
between knowledge and theory on the one hand,
and public purpose on the other.

Fredrick Mosher

Code enforcement is not a profession in the strict meaning of the word. The dictionary defines profession as "a calling requiring specialized knowledge and often long and intensive academic preparation."[1] As it is practiced today, code enforcement does not require much specialized knowledge, nor is it expected that an officer will have considerable academic background. A theorist of public administration, Dwight Waldo, wrote that "a profession, indeed a well-developed occupation, has an ethos that acts to shape the values and behavior of members."[2] Code enforcement does not have a well-articulated ethos as, for example, those in medicine or jurisprudence have. Another true sign of a profession, noted political scientist James Q. Wilson, is that some of

---

[1] Merriam-Webster's Collegiate Dictionary, 10th Edition.
[2] Dwight Waldo. The Enterprise of Public Administration: A Summary View. Novato, Ca: Chandler & Sharp Publishers, Inc., 1980, p. 105.

its members will systematically contribute through writing and research to the common knowledge of their field. Analyzing the work of police officers, Wilson concluded that by this standard the police are only sub-professionals.[3] Likewise, code enforcement officers cannot be called professionals either because they do not typically write in depth about their work or do scholarly research to contribute to their field of knowledge.

By these standards, code enforcement, therefore, is not a profession and possibly may never be. Yet in recent decades code enforcement has become a primary line of work for an increasing number of people throughout the United States; it has developed, and is still developing, into a recognizable feature in local government. And although it has only recently begun to be identified as a distinct field with its boundaries still blurry, for the purposes of this book I will make a simplifying assumption that code enforcement *is* an occupation in its own right. As physicist Stephen Barr explained, making a simplifying assumption in science is a necessity in order to study natural systems.[4]

But why should one study code enforcement in the first place? The argument of this book is that code enforcement makes for a captivating subject because of its very existence. The just-noted similarity between the police and code enforcement will be explored in more detail later,

---

[3] James Q. Wilson. <u>Varieties of Police Behavior: The Management of Law and Order in Eight Communities</u>. Cambridge, Mass.: Harvard University Press, 1968, p. 29.

[4] Making simplifying assumptions is necessary to do, writes Barr, "because real physical systems are far too complex to study exactly. For example, if one wants to understand the motion of a billiard ball, it makes sense for many purposes to treat the ball as if it were a perfect sphere of infinite rigidity. To treat it exactly would mean worrying about every microscopic scratch on its surface, its chemical composition, and all sorts of other details. Indeed, it would ultimately mean keeping track of every one of its atoms, which would be impossible in practice. [...] A vital part of scientific training is learning how to make sensible and useful approximations." Stephen M. Barr. <u>Modern Physics and Ancient Faith.</u> Notre Dame, Ind.: University of Notre Dame Press, 2003, p. 269.

but for now let us note that the police have existed for many years, yet the name "code enforcement" appeared only recently. If we recall that the issue of how much to police a community has from the early years of this country involved finding a balance between communal order and individual liberty, is it not important to understand why an *additional* form of policing has come about? What if in the appearance of code enforcement, we witness an enlargement of the state police powers?

If you agree with me that studying code enforcement is important, the next question is, Can it really be studied? How does one study a subject in social or political sciences where everything is so fluid? In Western philosophical tradition, to study a subject means first to distinguish the subject from its environment. In this spirit dating back to the philosophers of Ancient Greece, one begins by asking, What exactly is this thing we are examining? What is its definition? What are the boundaries that separate it from the rest of the world? In studying code enforcement, we too must ask, How can we define it? Can we draw a firm line around it and say, "This is where code enforcement begins, and this is where it ends"?

It is never easy to compress the variety of human activities into a single mold and give it a name, but an attempt to draw the circle and define code enforcement presents some special difficulties. The first difficulty is that there is often no hard line to draw between code enforcement and other related occupations. For instance, in the minds of many, code enforcement is related to housing inspection or health inspection. There are good reasons for this confusion: code enforcement has developed primarily out of these two fields, and it bears familiar traits inherited from both. In some instances, code enforcement duplicates many duties that housing and health inspectors still perform. In addition, code enforcement deals with fire prevention and fire safety too. Code officers often consult and enforce the Fire Code, and in this way they do what fire inspectors do. Code enforcement officers not infrequently regulate human behavior. Enforcing noise violations, smoking in public places, or business operations, for example, officers compel people to change the way they behave—directly and immediately. In this, they act like the police.

The second difficulty in drawing the circle around code enforcement is that its activities occur under different names and in different departments. I use "code enforcement" as the most common, but the same or very similar functions come under various other names. Local governments use "code enforcement" interchangeably with "code compliance," "community preservation," "neighborhood preservation," "community enhancement," "environmental quality," "neighborhood services," and "community revitalization." Likewise, code enforcement is found in many different departments: building and safety, planning, environmental services, public works, public safety, neighborhood services, housing, fire, or police. Accordingly, the staff performing code enforcement duties may be called zoning, building, housing, public works, or environmental inspectors or investigators, community compliance officers; they may also be called municipal, business license, community preservation, and bylaw officers, or (my favorite) community revitalization specialists. Some of them wear casual business attire, others wear distinctive uniforms. In some California cities, for example, code enforcement officers are almost indistinguishable from the police; in addition to uniforms with the police department patches, they carry handcuffs, batons, and even firearms. They are not sworn officers enforcing penal or vehicle codes, but they need all this equipment for personal protection while administering municipal and building codes. Distinguishing code enforcement in all these various and overlapping groups is not an easy task.

The third difficulty is that even if we could draw the line around code enforcement to separate it from related occupations, we would quickly discover that the line was constantly changing. It would be open and permeable, because depending on the current priorities, code enforcement duties could expand to include new laws or shrink to abandon others. They could also shift between code enforcement and other agencies, like the police, animal control, health, parking enforcement, or be outsourced to private companies. So again, should we attempt to draw a line separating code enforcement from other regulatory agencies, it would be forever unstable and blurry.

Given all these difficulties, can code enforcement be studied as a stand-alone subject? How can we be sure that it even exists?

3
CODE ENFORCEMENT EXISTS AND THRIVES

How can we be sure that code enforcement exists? There are several recent trends that, to me, show its existence as an identifiable field, although a dynamic one that is expanding, solidifying, breaking apart, and professionalizing all at the same time. The trends are four: the change in language, the number of people identifying themselves as code enforcement, the appearance of professional organizations; and the emergence of specialized education and ranking in code enforcement.

The first trend is the change in language. When a new word (or word combination) comes into use, it reflects a new phenomenon recognized by us language users. It would be impossible, of course, to determine how long the words "code enforcement" have been used to describe the process by which local governments uphold their laws. But in the last several decades these two words have come to describe a specific *regulatory unit* in local government. Note that the titles of "building inspector," "housing inspector," "health inspector," and "fire inspector" have not gone away; yet a new designation of "code enforcement officer" has appeared and gained acceptance. One could not know how common the words were in the pre-internet times, but a simple Google search for "code enforcement" at the time of writing yields millions of hits. The majority are websites of American cities describing the operation of their code enforcement units; others are job announcements seeking code enforcement officers. Similar searches made by the author in 2002-2003 resulted in 800-1000 hits.

The second trend is the appearance of personnel employed, not as building or health, or public works inspectors, but specifically as code enforcement officers. For example, the City of Los Angeles, one of the largest municipalities in the country, has had one group of code enforcement officers in the Housing Department, another group in the Building and Safety Department, and a third in the Bureau of Street Services. The much smaller City of West Hollywood in California, located on less than two square miles and has 36,000 residents has code enforcement staff of seventeen. We should note that these positions exist in addition to building and safety, fire, public works, law or parking enforcement staff. Code enforcement officers are employed not only by governments but also by private firms contracting with the government. These firms provide various consulting, engineering, and regulatory services, and along with plan checkers, engineers, and building inspectors, they seek and hire—distinctly and separately—code enforcement officers.

The third trend concerns the forming of professional organizations throughout the United States. The California Association of Code Enforcement Officers (CACEO) has 2,200 members, most of whom call themselves and are employed as code enforcement officers. Almost every other state has its own code enforcement association, and on the national level there is the American Association of Code Enforcement (AACE) whose membership collectively represents all 50 states, the District of Columbia, and Canada. An important fact is that all these professional associations began forming in the 1980s: in California, two associations were formed in 1986 (SCACEO) and in 1995 (CACE); in Texas, the association formed in 1985; in Michigan, in 1992; in Arkansas, in 1998; in Oregon, in 1995. The national organization

(AACE) formed in 1988. These three trends show code enforcement solidifying into a distinct field.

The fourth trend is the ongoing effort to provide occupational education and certification. In some cases, the state offers training and certification for code enforcement officers (the State of Maine's Office of Fire Marshal is one example). But mostly certification is done by the professional associations mentioned above. Their programs vary in scope and intensity. The associations in Georgia and Kansas, for example, at some point offered 48 hours of training, while a California association had four modules, each consisting of five full-day classes making a total of 160 hours. Aside from the basic, intermediate, and advanced modules for officers, the California association offered supervisory and managerial modules. The national AACE offers certifications as Code Enforcement Administrator and Master Code Enforcement Professional. The growing demand to prepare for supervisory and managerial jobs in code enforcement is a relatively recent development. Before, code enforcement officers were usually part of other divisions, such as building and safety or planning. Now, code enforcement divisions are common; thus, to become a manager, an appropriate supervisory certification can be useful. To strengthen their legitimacy in providing education, the associations often work with established institutions of higher learning. The Georgia Association of Code Enforcement, for example, provides training under the auspices of the University of Georgia; the California association has offered classes through community colleges; the Texas association works with University of Texas. While all the classes (and the membership itself) are voluntary, the certifications acquired through them are looked upon seriously by those who hire. In the absence of an established tradition of education, these voluntarily acquired certifications are viewed as an objective way to judge the candidate's qualifications.

Apart from education, code enforcement associations are active in lobbying for legislative agendas important to their membership. The

California Penal Code, for example, has been amended to include code enforcement officers in the list of occupations (next to police officers and firefighters) whose members receive additional protection against violence. A bill adding code enforcement officers to the home address confidentiality category has also been advanced through the legislative advocacy of the California association of code enforcement.

The above trends show code enforcement gradually solidifying into a field. As the field grows in size and complexity, however, there is the inevitable tendency to break apart and subdivide. It is always the case that when an organization or a field of knowledge becomes too large, it breaks into areas of specialization. In code enforcement, the subdivision may be seen as occurring *horizontally* (where the field breaks into smaller areas of specialized knowledge) and *vertically* (where the field develops different occupational ranks among officers).

The horizontal subdivision into specialized areas of enforcement may not be obvious in smaller cities. Where code enforcement staff is limited to one or two persons, they by necessity become generalists, enforcing a variety of code violations. The same officer will handle illegal business signs, prohibited noise, property maintenance, unlicensed street vendors, unpermitted garage sales, conditional use permits, abandoned vehicles, and even street parking. In a big city where more staff is available, officers become specialists. The City of Los Angeles, for example, has street inspectors, residential housing inspectors, home occupation inspectors, abandoned vehicle inspectors, and zoning inspectors. West Hollywood has had officers specializing in housing inspections and short-term rentals. This, as I said, shows the breaking of the field horizontally.

The vertical breaking can be seen through the stratification of code enforcement personnel, with new titles that simply weren't there before. In the 1980s, when the title "code enforcement officer" became common, the rank of "officer" (or inspector or investigator) was the only available job description. Today, various levels of jobs are available in code enforcement. Depending on experience, one may be hired as a manager, supervisor, senior code enforcement officer, code enforcement officer I or II, reserve code enforcement officer, code enforcement technician, code enforcement officer trainee, code enforcement aid, and the like. One example of such stratification comes from West Hollywood. In 1996, this boutique city had only four officers, who were part of the Building and Safety Division and reported, along with building inspectors, to the building official. In 2023, West Hollywood Code Enforcement is a division of its own. It has a manager, two supervisors, two senior officers, eight regular officers, a code enforcement technician, and a staff assistant. This increase in numbers cannot be explained through ordinary urban growth: West Hollywood is land-locked, and its size and population have not changed and cannot change. What changed, however, was the level of community demand that prompted the creation of additional weekend and night shifts, requiring additional staff, which in turn created the stratified ranks.

These four trends just mentioned allow us to make a reasonable assumption that code enforcement does exist as a distinct field, and it can be observed and studied. To be sure, the field is in flux and its boundaries are imprecise. But the same can be said about any social phenomenon. Should we give up studying code enforcement, we might as well give up studying culture, art, music, and politics. All of them are open systems whose limits are only nominal.

Now that we have agreed that code enforcement exists and, assuming it is a relatively new field, the question is, Why did code enforcement appear?

Trying to answer such a question can be difficult. A social phenomenon, especially one as open as we have described it, must result from a multitude of causes. How would we find them? The methodology of this book is simple. We will identify the essence of the phenomenon as we understand it today. Then we will look into the past to see if we can find when the same essence (even if under a different name) first appeared and what prompted its appearance. Then, perhaps, we can attempt to answer the why question.

We should not expect to find only one explanation. Causality does not have to be a single line, but can be a bundle of lines, like a filament consisting of many fibers. We should be prepared to discover that our phenomenon, code enforcement, resulted from several causes that came together at some point and acquired the name under which we know it today. In the following pages, then, after we identify the essence of what we understand as code enforcement today, we will trace it back to the early days of several American cities. Was the essence then and there as it is here and now? Did the cities have anything resembling code enforcement in their early governments?

4

CODE ENFORCEMENT AS MAINTENANCE OF ORDER

Modern code enforcement deals with a wide variety of issues. Officers enforce almost the entire municipal codes, which include hundreds of pages of laws on land use, housing, noise, environmental protection, business operation, animal control, and health and fire safety. Consider two California cities. In the City of San Jose, officers enforce

- Conditions of an existing structure that constitute a clear and present danger to the public.
- Building Code violations (building, plumbing, electrical, mechanical, etc.), including construction or change of occupancy without permits.
- Minimum standards for safe and sanitary housing.
- Zoning Ordinance requirements for structures (such as use, location, configuration and size) and land use requirements.
- Weeds on private, developed property.
- Swimming pool fences.
- Graffiti.
- Signs, including signs in the public right-of-way, failure to have required permits, illegal inflatable displays, balloons and pennants.
- Inoperable and abandoned vehicles on public streets and private property.
- Blight on private and public properties (old furniture, car parts, appliances, etc.).
- Lawn parking.
- Early set out of yard trimmings.
- Illegal dumping.
- Smoking in enclosed public places.
- Water waste.

In the City of Anaheim, as another example, officers

o   enforce the Anaheim Municipal Code and other related State codes.
o   conduct business license inspections.
o   investigate and conduct housing, nuisance and zoning code inspections in residential, industrial and commercial areas.
o   oversee the City's graffiti removal and prevention programs.
o   conduct anti-scavenging enforcement.
o   [do] street vendor enforcement [and]
o   taxicab enforcement.

However diverse the enforcement duties listed above may be, they have one common denominator: they all deal with conditions that upset a pre-existing order. The officer's job is to restore it. When a violation occurs, communal order is infringed upon, and the officer—whether she is stopping a loud party, ordering the removal of weeds or graffiti or forcing the repair of a leaky faucet—is restoring an upset order. For there was once a quiet neighborhood; there was once a clean wall and green grass, and the faucet did not leak. That was order.[5]

The same is true for the police which, of course, serves as the model for much of what code enforcement does. The main purpose of police

---

[5] This line of thinking owes to James Q. Wilson. "Most criminal laws define *acts* (murder, rape, speeding, possessing narcotics), which are held to be illegal; people may disagree as to whether the act should be illegal, as they do with respect to narcotics, for example, but there is little disagreement as to what the behavior in question consists of. Laws regarding disorderly conduct and the like assert, usually by implication, that there is a *condition* ("public order") that can be diminished by various actions. The difficulty, of course, is that public order is nowhere defined and can never be defined unambiguously because what constitutes order is a matter of opinion and convention, not a state of nature. (An unmurdered person, an un-raped woman, and an unpossessed narcotic can be defined so as to be recognizable to any reasonable person.)" James Q. Wilson. <u>Varieties of Police Behavior: The Management of Law and Order in Eight Communities</u>. Cambridge, Mass.: Harvard University Press, 1968, pp. 21-22.

work is the maintenance of peace and order (while detection of criminals and charging them with crime are only secondary duties). This is how Thomas Dye, for example, describes the role of police:

> The police are on the front line of society's efforts to resolve *conflict*. Indeed, instead of a legal or law enforcement role, the police are more likely to adopt a *peacekeeping role*. They are generally lenient in their arrest practices; that is, they use their arrest powers less often than the law allows. Rather than arresting people, the police prefer first *to reestablish order* [emphasis added].[6]

Compare this with the stress on the importance of compliance rather than punishment formulated by Joseph M. Schilling and James B. Hare in their book *Code Enforcement: A Comprehensive Approach*. "Compliance" in their context means the re-establishment of order:

> Compliance is the primary objective of comprehensive code enforcement; penalties and punishment are secondary. Public policy goals, implementation of adopted regulations, and resolution of enforcement cases are accomplished through compliance. While the imposition of penalties, punishment, and incarceration may be justified as a deterrent to crimes involving personal behavior, a code enforcement official is usually more interested in correcting a physical deficiency in a place or structure.[7]

What Schilling and Hare call a "physical deficiency" stands for upset order. For there is an implicit presumption that the "place or structure" had once been in an *orderly* state which is violated by the physical deficiency. By eliminating the deficiency—by gaining compliance in Schilling and Hare's terms—the orderly state is re-established. Even

---

[6] Thomas R. Dye. <u>Understanding Public Policy</u>. Upper Saddle River, NJ: Prentice Hall, 2002, p. 67.

[7] Joseph M. Schilling and James B. Hare. <u>Code Enforcement: A Comprehensive Approach.</u> Point Arena, Ca: Solano Press Books, 1994, p. 7.

when the code enforcement officer deals with personal behavior—for example, a gardener using a loud leaf blower, which is a violation in some cities—the first thing the officer does by approaching the gardener is, in fact, ask him to stop using the machine. Whether a citation or warning is issued is secondary to the main purpose—restoring peace and quiet. Once the machine is off, the order has been restored.

The same applies to the health inspector, another cousin of the code officer: she performs the same order-restoration-and-maintenance function. When a dilapidated apartment building was built, it did not have rats or roaches, its sewage system did not leak, there was no trash, its paint was not peeling, and its windows were not broken. It is the health inspector's job to have those original conditions restored. So is the job of the fire inspector, who orders, for example, that the building's exits not be blocked—just the way they were when the building was built; that the smoke alarms be operational—just as they were when new; that the windows allow quick emergency exit—just as they were designed to be. The fire inspector makes sure that this orderly state, present when the building was new, is maintained.

It is clear, then, that as an instrument of order restoration and maintenance, code enforcement is closely related to the police, fire, and health departments. It is also clear how it differs from building inspection. It is not understandable when code enforcement is confused with building inspection—to call someone who inspects buildings a building inspector is natural. In today's municipality, however, there is a fundamental distinction. "Building inspector" means one who oversees new construction. A code officer, on the other hand, is the one who comes after. He sees to it that already built buildings are maintained. The difference is again in how these two relate to communal order. When the building inspector comes to a construction site, order has not been created yet—it exists only in drawings. The building inspector makes sure the building is built according to the drawings. He helps create order. Once the building is built, the building inspector's job is over. Now begins the job of the code enforcement officer to see that the newly created order is maintained as it was meant to be. This is why the nature of code enforcement work is mostly reactive. There is nothing for her to do until and unless the established order is violated. In an ideal world, code enforcement would not be needed.

If the above is true, the subject of the study can now be defined in the following way:

Code enforcement is part of the police powers exercised by the local government to maintain order as it is defined by the given community.

There may be, of course, other definitions, two of which, for example, can be found in the Schiller and Hare book.[8] The one I am proposing stresses three points that are important for this study. The first is that code enforcement is an order maintenance function. The second is that code enforcement is considered in its context: it is one instrument among many in the communal toolbox. Others include the police, fire department, health department, environmental protection department, parking enforcement, public works inspectors, and whatever other regulatory mechanisms the community needs and implements. The third point emphasizes the community as the defining agent of what its order will be at a given time.

---

[8] "Traditionally [code enforcement] has been a process whereby local governments use various techniques to gain compliance with duly adopted regulations such as land use and zoning ordinances, health and housing codes, sign standards, and uniform building and fire codes." The authors further reiterate that "[c]ode enforcement is defined as the process by which public agencies gain compliance with those laws, regulations, and permits over which they have authority." Schilling and Hare, Code Enforcement: A Comprehensive Approach. Solano Press, Point Arena CA, 1995, pp. 3 and 4.

The stance a community takes towards its own order is crucial, for its very existence and well-being depend on how it defines order, how sensitive it is to threats to order, and how aggressively it goes about defending it. But what we call communal order is not a single idea that has been developed once and frozen in time. Rather, it is a set of interacting ideas that change over time. We should not be surprised if we discover that as the community evolves, its understanding of order also evolves. The community define and re-define order all the time.

Order can be thought of as a set of ideas envisioning the best possible development for everything under human control that may happen *in* the community or *to* the community, and that may potentially go wrong. Communal order may include, for example, interactions between community members, interactions between community members and their rulers, interactions between community members and the outsiders, the division of the available land, the condition of the structures on the land, the building and maintenance of the protective wall surrounding the community, and the like. Communal order expresses what residents want their community to be if they could make it perfect. Communal order is an ideal state of events.

To keep things as close as possible to the ideal, the community takes two basic steps. The first step is that the ideal order is captured in laws (that is, in words put on paper or chiseled on a rock), prohibiting conditions and behavior that are threatening to the ideal. As the community changes over time—growing or declining, being pressured from the outside or torn from the inside—new threats to the ideal arise. They may be real or imaginary, they may be coming from within or without, they may be physical or emotional, but once they are perceived and identified, the community articulates new laws. It seeks to stop those threats; it prohibits conditions and behavior that contributes to them. It now re-defines the ideal. It says, in effect, that the ideal now must exclude such and such things in addition to what has been excluded before. They were not considered threatening, but now they are. The list of the threats has grown. The definition of order has expanded.

The second step is obvious: the laws need to be enforced. A human being charged with observing and stopping violations has to be there. It was not uncommon in Colonial America, as we will see, that new laws were enforced by volunteers. Over time, however, as laws multiplied and enforcement became a full-time job needing specialized knowledge, volunteers turned professionals. New occupations, new names of enforcers emerged.

In the following pages, we will see how American communities recognized first threats to order, passed their first laws, and designated their first enforcers. We will notice that the definition of order would change over time due mostly to urban growth; more people moving in and roaming around the town felt like a menace to communal well-being. The swelling population of the American ports where they first arrived gave life to regulatory agencies as we know them today. New York, Boston, and San Francisco offer us prime examples of how colonial settlements grew into communities, communities into towns, and towns into cities. It was there, as we will discover, that the police officer, health inspector, fire inspector, and building inspector first came to be. And it was there that many duties performed today by code enforcement originated.

5

THE BEGINNING OF ORDER IN NEW AMSTERDAM

What we know today as the great city of New York began its history in 1609 when the English explorer Henry Hudson landed on Manhattan Island. He was employed by a Dutch trading company, and the company's first trading posts were set up on the island a few years later. In 1626, Peter Minuit, a merchant running the new Dutch settlement, traded the entire island from the local indigenous people for some twenty-four dollars' worth of beads and ribbons. A fort was built at the southern tip of the island, and the settlement was named New Amsterdam (changed to New York in 1664 when it came under English control).[9]

We are fortunate to have the colony's early historic records. Examining them, we can see how it all began: how the colony grew; how it worked to establish an orderly life; how it adopted its first rules; and where it found its first enforcers. In this small exemplar of American colonial

---

[9] Elson, Henry W. <u>History of the United States of America</u>. The Macmillan company, 1918, p. 133.

life, we can see in detail what kind of problems they dealt with and how, in response to them, there appeared the prototypes of modern municipal occupations: police, fire, and building inspectors. We should not be surprised if we recognize in their long-past ways of life many features familiar to us today.

New Amsterdam was governed by a Director-General and a five-member Council, similar to how a small city today is governed by a five-member city council and a city manager. The settlement was indeed small. Its nucleus was a group of 270 men, women, and children who arrived in 1625. These were primarily families, and families are naturally stable and orderly units. What interests us is how they, living as one settlement, established communal order among themselves. At which point did these internally orderly groups, augmented as they would be over time by new arrivals, become externally disorderly? At which point did they have to undertake collective efforts to establish order on the communal level?

The families that formed the nucleus of New Amsterdam came on their own wish, and they intended to stay. This self-selected group of inhabitants had a "peaceful and orderly disposition" that made any police regulations simply unnecessary. Not even a guard was on duty at night, wrote Augustine Costello, and the norms of propriety were held so high that it was a sign of bad morals to be out after nine o'clock.[10] The small and homogeneous population of the settlement where everybody knew each other explains, of course, why the typical crimes associated with modern urban life were non-existent.

As the settlement grew, however, among the residents began appearing Dutch freebooters and other transient characters from the nearby Gulf islands. In the words of Costello, their personalities and vagrant modes

---

[10] Augustine E. Costello. <u>Our police protectors: history of the New York police from the earliest period to the present time</u>. NY: C.F. Roper, 1885, p. 3.

of life did not prepare them for settled life or for patiently enduring personal insults, and the incidents of drunkenness and even knife drawings became frequent.[11] In addition to the sailors and adventurers, New Amsterdam began attracting traders from other parts of the world who were not Dutch. Within only a dozen years after its founding, the colony was already known for its remarkable cultural and religious tolerance, especially when compared with the Puritan colonies in Massachusetts Bay. It quickly became the most ethnically mixed settlement where an impressed visitor reported hearing eighteen different languages.[12] But all this diversity and transiency could not but challenge communal order, and the first symbol of a penal system in New Amsterdam appeared in 1632. It was a whipping post set up at the water's edge.

But who would bring the culprit to the whipping post, we may ask? Whose job was it to police New Amsterdam? We can trace the American prototype of what we today call the police to a special official in the colonial administration, his Dutch title was *Schout Fiscal*. His duties were multiple: institute and conduct council's proceedings, enforce laws, ordinances, resolutions and military regulations, and protect the rights, domains and jurisdiction of the Dutch West India Company. The official conducted prosecutions and suits, both criminal and civil, except that he could not arrest any person on a criminal charge unless he received a complaint or himself witnessed someone commit a crime. Today, his job would be split between police officer, bailiff, and district attorney. But that was not all. He also inspected the papers of vessels arriving or leaving New Amsterdam and, to prevent smuggling, watched over loading and unloading of cargoes. The Schout Fiscal received no salary for his services but was "compensated by certain fees allowed him in particular cases."[13]

---

[11] Ibid., pp. 3-4.

[12] Alan Taylor. <u>American Colonies</u>. NY: Viking Penguin, 2001, p. 255.

[13] Costello, pp. 2-3 and 8.

In 1651, the Director General (city manager) attempted to appoint a *ratel-wacht*, a team of night patrolmen. His innovation was not popular, however, and the team soon disbanded. What prompted the attempt was not merely the need to maintain order at night and watch out for fires, but in addition to apprehend a possible attack by New England colonists, an event the town considered imminent. After another failed attempt in 1654 by the Director, the rattle-watch team was finally put in operation in 1658. Eight watchmen carrying rattles were on duty from nine at night till early morning. Although they were paid some cash and given free firewood for their services, this was not their primary job. The rattle-watch duty was mandatory for all male citizens, and each household paid fifteen *stuyvers* to support the service.[14] We can recognize here the beginning of a paid police force in America—at least in its night patrol function.

It was not only the fear of fire or attack that made night patrol attractive, but also the now-increased population of New Amsterdam. By 1656 it reached 1000 people. As is always the case, a large number of people who do not recognize each other's faces prompts the need for protection, and therefore for the police. But the increased population created other concerns too. The thousand residents of New Amsterdam lived in approximately 120 houses. We should not be surprised to learn that given the increase yet another job description appeared.

It had happened even before the night patrol. In 1647, the colonial administration created three positions they called *surveyors*. Today, we would call them city inspectors. The official *Records of New Amsterdam* tell us what prompted the move. According to the *Records*, members of the administration complained about houses built in a "disorderly manner." They noticed that some owners extended their lots beyond property lines; that others neglected to develop the lots granted to them;

---

[14] Costello, p. 11 and Earle, p. 77.

and that pigpens and outhouses were placed on the public streets. To curb all these signs of disorder, the administration deemed it necessary to pass a new regulation and appoint three surveyors to enforce it. The surveyors were respectable members of the community who had undertaken these new responsibilities in addition to their regular jobs. Lubbert van Dincklagen was an attorney and judge; Poulus Leendersen was a horse carriage master; and Cornelis van Tienhoven was the administration secretary. The new regulation empowered the three men to condemn improper and disorderly buildings, fences, palisades, post, rails and such, and prevent their erection in the future. "We therefore command and warn all and everybody of our subjects," the new regulation read, "who henceforth intend to build or put palisades around their gardens or lots in or near the City of New Amsterdam, that nobody shall dare do or undertake it without previous knowledge, consent of and inspection by the above named appointed surveyors, under penalty of 25 Carolusguilders and destruction of what may have been built or set up."[15] Thus, for the first time on American soil the idea of building permit was enshrined in law.[16]

Consider how this early government regulation related to order. In 1647, New Amsterdam's communal order was not set up yet; the town's basic physical features—its parcels of land, the layout of its street—were still being established. Yet, from their language expressing what the administration was against, we know what it was after. It denounced "disorderly manner"; therefore, it sought order. It sought an ideal state

---

[15] *The Records of New Amsterdam I, 4*, quoted in James Ford, _Slums and Housing: History, Conditions, Policy._ Harvard University Press, 1936, V. I, p. 28. Henceforth the spelling of the *Records* has been modernized.

[16] Compare how today's International Building Code expresses the same idea: "Any owner or owner's authorized agent who intends to construct, enlarge, alter, repair, move, demolish or change the occupancy of a building or structure, or to erect, install, enlarge, alter, repair, remove, convert or replace any electrical, gas, mechanical or plumbing system, the installation of which is regulated by this code, or to cause any such work to be performed, shall first make application to the building official and obtain the required permit."

of affairs. The administration and its surveyors had an image in their minds of what New Amsterdam should be: its streets straight and clean, its pigpens and outhouses on private land only, its lots developed and houses built orderly. We can now see this seemingly unremarkable document dated 1647 as an important milestone: it was one of the earliest government regulations on American soil, establishing communal order and creating a new occupation we now call city inspector.

We should note some characteristic features of this new regulation and its enforcers. We note first that by modern standards the surveyors' job was rather broad. In our time it would be several different professions. They were surveyors in today's meaning of the word, that is, measuring land and establishing property lines. But they also consented to the construction of new houses, which is what today's planner, plan checker, and building inspector do. They also condemned illegally built houses, fences, posts, and palisades, which are the jobs of today's building inspector or code enforcement officer.

We note second the ambiguity of the surveyors' payment. It is not clear from the sources that came down to us if the surveyors were paid for their services. From what we know from other history, however, the common practice of the time was to assign such *honorary duties* as surveying to the richest members of the community. That was for the simple reason that the rich would be less inclined to bribery. It is clear, therefore, why surveying was not and could not be their primary occupation. After fulfilling their honorary duties, attorney Dincklagen would go back to law, master Leendersen to making horse carriages, and secretary Tienhoven to calligraphy.

But something must have been amiss in this setup. The strong "nobody shall dare" must not have had the desired effect at the time because the same regulation had to be repeated almost verbatim nine years later. The new 1656 regulation re-stated the old one: "Nobody shall erect houses, corners, fences, gates, or such like, before first having called the Surveyors to the place and received their survey and approbation, under penalty." Even this order did not work, wrote historian James Ford, because the fines were too lenient or they were not levied or executed.[17]

It is not difficult to imagine why the fines might not have been levied or executed. A New Amsterdam surveyor's job was prone to have a conflict of interest. He was a government enforcer ordering people to stop building houses and collecting fines from them. But he was also a member of a small community where his own livelihood depended on the very neighbors he was to fine. Under the circumstances, the surveyor probably tended to display as much goodwill and as much leniency as possible. In today's code enforcement language, he was seeking compliance, not punishment.

Without strict enforcement, however, the law was toothless, and only a year later, in 1657, a change was enacted: the surveyor was no longer a volunteer. His status was elevated, and his payment spelled out. As before, he was to impose a fine but now the amount was split with "one third to go to the Officer, who is to collect it, two thirds into the City treasury."[18] For the first time on American soil a government enforcer was paid for his services. Although this change would be unlikely to alleviate his conflict of interest if he had another job elsewhere, it was meant to make the surveyors more independent. His livelihood was now meant to be paid for by this job only, so that he did not have to work elsewhere, for example, as a carriage maker or scribe. A portion of the fine going to the surveyor's pocket was meant to create an independent professional.

---

[17] Ford, pp. 30-31.
[18] Ibid., pp. 34-35.

Finally, we should note the peculiarity of the language of the regulation. It does not define "disorderly." It does not explain how the surveyors would determine what kind of construction constituted a violation. It must have been left to their discretion to decide what was orderly and what was not. The reason I focus on this is that the vagueness of language found in old codes should not surprise us. Words such as "disorderly," "improper," "unsightly" or "offensive" do not and cannot express a specific standard. They express our *aspirations* to live in a world that would be orderly, proper, sightly, and inoffensive. But aspirations cannot be expressed with any specificity; they cannot be spelled out except in words, mostly adjectives and adverbs, that are vague.

We recognize this challenge as something very familiar to us today. Working in code enforcement, we are challenged by the vagueness of our property maintenance codes every day. What does it mean, for example, to have "accumulation of trash" on the property? How much trash constitutes "accumulation"—a few pieces of paper on the ground or a two-foot pile? And what if the property is a construction site with building materials and debris strewn around—how much trash does it take to be in violation there? We often lament the law's vagueness; we often wish that our codes would be more specific, for this would surely make our jobs easier. We often think that modern technical codes (such as building, plumbing, mechanical, or electrical) are what all codes should be like, because their standards are expressed clearly, in numbers. When a technical code says, for example, that a gap between this and that should be no more than six inches, it is easy to enforce. Anyone with a measuring tape can see if there is a violation or not. There is no controversy and no argument. But when a code says, as in the example above, that there should be no accumulation of trash or that something should be in "good working order," it is up to the officer's judgment to decide what a violation is. The building inspector carries around his measuring tape. The code enforcement officer carries around his judgment. This can be both a blessing and a curse, but this is also what makes the job so interesting. We will return to this topic at the end of the book, but for now the point is that the vagueness of law is the norm, not an exception, and we can see the earliest examples of such vagueness as far back as in Colonial America.

We have just discussed that already in 1647 disorderly construction of houses and fences was recognized as a threat to communal order. At that time the order was only emerging, for many lots were still empty. A year later when some lots had been already developed and houses built on them, a new threat to communal order emerged—fires. This was a threat to the already-existing order, and from that moment on, much enforcement effort would be directed towards the *maintenance* of order, rather than its creation. So, in 1648, a year after the three surveyors were appointed, another government enforcer appeared. He was the prototype of what we today call the fire inspector, and his title in Dutch was *brandt-meester*—the firemaster of chimneys. The appointment came, read the official decree, because it "has been noticed and seen [...] that some careless people neglect, to have their chimneys properly swept and that they do not take care of their fires, whereby lately fires broke out in two houses and further troubles may be expected in the future, the more so, as most of the houses here in New Amsterdam are built of wood and roofed with reeds, also as in some house the chimneys are of wood, which is very dangerous."[19]

The new law also decreed that "no wooden or merely plastered chimneys shall be put into any house," which was one of the earliest regulations prohibiting a then-common practice in building construction. The law stipulated that those chimneys already in use could remain as-is until further orders and at the discretion of the firemasters, granting what we today call grandfathering rights to existing buildings. The newly appointed firemasters could visit, whenever they please, all houses to check if the chimneys were clean. If they found

---

[19] *The Records of New Amsterdam*, p.5 quoted in Ford v.1 p. 28.

them neglected, they could collect a fine right on the spot for "each chimney so found foul and condemned." The fine would be "applied to the purchase of fire ladder, hooks and buckets."[20]

To the modern American ear accustomed to the idea of constitutional protection of one's home, that the firemasters could "visit, whenever they please, the chimneys in all houses" may sound drastic. But even in the pre-Constitution times this government invasion of privacy was much disliked. Alice Morse Earle in her book *Colonial Days in Old New York* wrote that the residents considered this effort—undertaken, to be sure, for the sake of their own safety—to be espionage over their hearthstones. Housewives were especially vocal about "the snooping" taking place in their kitchens, and they abused the firemaster by calling him a little cock, booted and spurred, and other demeaning names.[21] Firemasters were appreciated in New Amsterdam even less than surveyors.

We may wonder why fire safety was such a concern, however, considering that many lots were still empty, and houses were far away from each other. With little danger of a fire affecting more than one house at a time, why was this legislative action needed? There could be several reasons. First, in the early settlement the building of a new house or rebuilding of a destroyed one was not an individual but a communal effort. (See, for example, Louis B. Wright's description of the Pilgrims building the first house in Plymouth in 1620.[22]) Second, when a family lost their home to fire, it became a burden for others, as the victims needed to be temporarily housed elsewhere. Third, when fires broke out, almost the entire community had to participate in suppressing it.

---

[20] *The Records of New Amsterdam*, quoted in Ford, p. 29.

[21] Alice Morse Earle. Colonial Days in Old New York. NY: Empire State Book Co., 1926, pp. 74-75.

[22] Louis B. Wright. The Atlantic Frontier: colonial American civilization, 1607-1763. NY: Alfred A. Knopf, 1947, pp. 107-108.

Alice Morse Earle provided a description of such communal effort—the bucket service brigade:

> As soon as an alarm of fire was given by shouts or bell-ringing, all citizens of all classes at once ran to the scene of the conflagration. All who owned buckets carried them, and from open windows other fire buckets were flung out on the streets by persons who were delayed for a few moments by any cause. The running crowd seized the buckets, and on reaching the fire a double line was made from the fire to the river. The buckets filled with water were passed up the line to the fire, the empty buckets down. Anyone who attempted to break the line was promptly soused with a bucket of water.[23]

A fire did not only affect the family whose house got burnt; it disrupted the normal flow of life for the whole settlement. This is why a later law imposed a double fine even on that hapless owner whose house had already suffered from fire.[24]

As new settlers arrived and the town grew, the threat of fire increased. New houses were built closer to each other—the European style—and even adjoining each other. Now fires were no longer simply disruptive to the normal flow of life. The fire in one home could jump from one house to another and ruin the whole block. This was the threat that led in 1657 to a new law announcing that all thatched roofs and faulty chimneys were to be removed within four months of notice; otherwise, a new tax would be levied on their owners.[25]

In the above examples we can see a recurring pattern: the recognition of a new threat leads to a new regulation, which leads to the appointment of a new enforcer. We see the same pattern in yet another example: how New Amsterdam handled its trash. It was noted by the administration

---

[23] Earle, pp. 76-77.
[24] Ford, p. 31.
[25] Ibid.

that many residents mishandled rubbish, filth, ashes, and dead animals "to the great inconvenience of the community and dangers arising from it." This led to a new type of decree in 1657 that was a prototype of modern sanitary regulations. The decree required the householders to keep the sidewalks in front of them clean, prohibited tossing trash into the streets and canal, designated places for trash collection, spelled out fines, and designated an enforcement officer:

> No one shall be allowed to throw any rubbish, filth ashes, oyster-shells, dead animal or anything like it, but they shall bring all such things to most convenient of the following places: near the City hall, near the gallows, near Hendrick the baker, and near Daniel Litsco, where signs to that effect shall be displayed, but not on the public streets under a penalty of 3 florins for the first offense, 6 florins for the second, and arbitrary punishment for the third. Furthermore, everybody is ordered to keep the streets clean before his house or lot under the preceding penalties. And that this be done, we herewith charge and command our Officer to execute this order after publication and to proceed against all transgressors, as in duty he is bound.[26]

The definition of communal order, as we can see, has now expanded: in addition to proper development of vacant lots and fire protection, it now included cleanliness.

Another pressing problem was domesticated animals. In his book *The Sanitary City*, Martin Melosi noted that animals played an integral part in pre-industrial America and lived side by side with people. Horses were used for transportation and work; cattle, hogs, turkeys, and chickens were bred for food; pigs and turkeys were "useful scavengers" as they fed on garbage; dogs and cats were kept as pets. All of them roamed public streets and private properties, leaving behind manure or,

---

[26] *The Records of New Amsterdam* quoted in Ford, p. 31 (edited for clarity).

sometimes, simply dying in the middle of the street.[27] The negative impact of having animals as part of life had to be balanced against the need to share space with them, and the first example of what we today would call animal control law appeared as early as 1648. As in the previous examples, some members of the colonial administration claimed that they saw daily and with their own eyes that the goats and hogs were causing great damage in orchards and gardens. Thus, the administration ordered that no hogs or goats were to be pastured in the middle of the town, unless they were behind fences that the goats could not jump over. Pasturing of goats in other places was permitted only with a herder. A goat found outside the fences or without a herder was to be confiscated and declared public property. "Let everybody hereby be warned and guard against loss," the law stated.[28] New Amsterdam's definition of communal order has now included animal control.

In this early period of New Amsterdam's development, we also find reports of the first, albeit unsuccessful, attempts to establish what would now be called zoning control. It was recognized early on that particular businesses had a negative effect on residents living nearby: noise from a blacksmith or smell from a tanner were obvious offenders. But could their separation from residences be made into law? At least one attempt was made but failed. The issue arose, as often happens, out of conflict between business and residents. In 1664, two neighbors appeared before the New Amsterdam Council to complain about a tannery that had been established between their properties. They feared that the water in their wells would be contaminated by the water seeping from the tannery's backyard where the skins were soaked, but most importantly they found unbearable the great stench coming from the tanning of skins. They requested that the Council forbid such business between their houses, especially the digging of the pit in which the skins would be soaked and washed. Unfortunately for them, the honorable

---

[27] Melosi, p. 19.

[28] *The Records of New Amsterdam* quoted in Ford, p. 29.

members of the council decreed in favor of the tanner, citing the rule of precedent: "as others have been allowed to make a tannery behind their house and lot, such cannot be forbidden."[29] What was felt to be a threat to communal order by some residents (the stench) was deemed acceptable to others (who probably lived further away).

The New Amsterdam administration may not have been able to stop the stench, but it did try to make the town quieter. Everyone entering the town walls and moving through the streets was required to ride his horse no faster than "foot-tap." The carters were required to dismount and walk at their horses' heads instead. Unnecessary shooting of firearms in the fortified town was prohibited too as the idle "fyring of pistells and gunns" was considered "ill-conveniants."[30] This was the beginning of government control over noise, which is one of the responsibilities of code enforcement in the modern city.

In 1653, the population of New Amsterdam was about eight hundred people; the area around the town, called New Netherlands, had about two thousand more. In the early years, the population growth was organic and moderate. But in 1653 a book was published in Holland that described the colony of New Amsterdam in such colorful terms that it produced a spike of interest. More immigrants arrived at the Hudson Valley, and by 1664 (around the time when it came under British control and was renamed New York) the Dutch population of New Netherlands increased by fivefold; it was now more than 10,000.[31]

The following chart provides a visual summary of how the adoption of new laws and regulations went parallel to the population growth in New Amsterdam and the area around it.

---

[29] Ford, p. 33.

[30] Earle, pp. 73-74.

[31] Henry William Elson. History of the United States of America. The MacMillan Company, New York, 1918, p. 137.

Year	Population	Order Maintenance Measure
1625	270	
1632		Whipping post set up
1647		Three surveyors appointed
1648		Animal control enacted; fire inspectors appointed
1651		1st failed attempt to appoint rattle-watch
1654	800	2nd failed attempt to appoint rattle-watch
1656	1000	Role of surveyors amplified
1657		Thatched roof, wooden chimneys prohibited; trash control and collection established
1658		Rattle-watch appointed
1664	10,000 +	Failed attempt at zoning control

***

The examples provided in this chapter show that over the course of approximately ten years, between 1647 and 1657, the colonial administration passed new regulations prohibiting one type of behavior after another. We can view their actions as the evidence of an expanded understanding of order. At the end of the decade, it included more items than in the beginning. First, it was the protection of public peace; second, it was the proper development of lots and orderly building; third, it was fire safety; fourth came sanitation; fifth was animal control; and sixth was noise. Simultaneously with the new additions emerged new enforcers: the Schout Fiscal, the rattle-watch, the surveyors, and the firemasters.

Of course, all these gradually added threats to order were not new to anyone. The residents of New Amsterdam came from Europe where they had been familiar with the same issues and attempted to resolve them through the same means. Keeping the streets clean and quiet was nothing new. But what New Amsterdam's example allows us to see is how a group of people starting a new life on a small parcel of land had first to create order, then to expand it, and finally to maintain it. As in a drop of seawater placed under the microscope shows the molecular structure of the whole ocean, New Amsterdam's experience shows how human beings create and protect orderly life.

These centuries-old examples also demonstrate the truth about the immutability of human nature. Manhattan Island today is nothing like New Amsterdam in 1625. And yet, people living there four hundred years ago faced challenges very similar to those of modern New Yorkers. They wanted to have their houses built orderly, and so do we. They were afraid of fires, and so are we. Their senses were offended by stench and trash, and so are ours. And they wanted their sleep uninterrupted at night as much as we do. Because the human body and its senses have not changed, our understanding of threats to order have not changed either. It is easy to see, then, how the enforcement duties that originated in New Amsterdam would continue in later places and later times. From behind the quaint Dutch titles emerge the familiar figures of modern city officials. The laws they passed are still on our books. This is why we do not live under thatched roofs and no goats roam our streets. The continuity is there because human nature does not change.

Nor does it change in its drive towards perfection. Since the New Amsterdam early regulations, many new laws have been passed and many new enforcers hired. Not only do we want order as much as people of New Amsterdam did, we seem to want more of it. We yearn to build upon *what is* and add to it *what can be*. We yearn to build a city upon a hill.

6
BOSTON WINE

Colonial Boston differed from New Amsterdam in that it had a more rigid religious culture and a more homogeneous population, yet its efforts to establish and maintain order were similar. After a brief recount of the similarities, we will focus mostly on one Boston regulation we did not see in New Amsterdam.

Settled in 1630, Boston had its first sanitary rules imposed in 1634. It prohibited residents from throwing garbage and fish near the common landing. A later regulation, also preventing the pollution of the harbor, came in 1647. In 1652, the town authorities began regulating the construction and placement of outhouses.[32] Also called a privy, an outhouse was a free-standing booth over a hole in the ground, usually made of wood and located as far away from the dwelling as possible. This regulation began the long list of sanitary laws that are still in existence today. Within the first year Boston also had, just like New

---

[32] Martin V. Melosi. <u>The Sanitary City: urban infrastructure in America from colonial times to the present.</u> Baltimore, Maryland: The Johns Hopkins University Press, 2000, pp. 20-21.

Amsterdam, regulations prohibiting thatched roofs and wooden chimneys.[33]

Yet Boston was different too. After all it was meant to be a city upon a hill, and it had high aspirations for public morals. Boston pioneered the earliest in America licensing of the sale of alcohol. The town administration did not prohibit what they called the houses of common entertainment, but it sought to regulate them. The administration acknowledged that it was "lawful liberty" to consume alcohol, but it wished to check the abuses coming from it "both by persons entertaining and persons entertained." To achieve that, the administration did what all administrations do: it set up a system of licensing. It proclaimed in 1648 that no person shall, at any time under any pretense or color whatsoever, sell wine, ale, beer, or distilled liquor, either privately in his house or out of doors in *small quantities*. One could only do so with approval of the Townsmen (modern city council) and having obtained a license issued by the local court. Punishment for not having a license was five pounds for every offense, or imprisonment at pleasure of the court.[34]

A merchant who obtained the license was to follow detailed guidelines as to how much to charge for wine and distilled liquor. In addition, he had the responsibility to control drunk behavior. No merchant, read the law, innkeeper, or tavern owner selling wine shall tolerate any person drinking to excess, or being drunk, in any wine-cellar, ship or vessel, or place where wine was sold. A first failure to control customers was

---

[33] Lawrence W. Kennedy. <u>Planning the City upon a Hill: Boston since 1630</u>. Amherst: University of Massachusetts Press, 1992, p. 16.

[34] <u>The Laws and Liberties of Massachusetts: reprinted from the copy of the 1648 edition in the Henry E. Huntington Library, with an introduction by Richard S. Dunn</u>. San Marino, Ca: The Henry E. Huntington Library, 1998, pp. 29-30 (language modernized for clarity).

punishable by ten shillings; the second, by double fines; for the third the merchant's license was revoked.[35]

One is tempted to think that it was the Puritan pessimistic view of the fallenness of human nature that certain behavior or practice (such as consuming alcohol) could not be prevented altogether. The way to deal with such evils was to allow them, but with conditions. Alcohol was not the only activity to be regulated. Boston also licensed food sales, butchery, and later the pawnshops. This began a long tradition of municipal regulation, on American soil, of trades that concerned public interest, that is, those commercial activities that have the potential to upset communal order but that cannot be prohibited.

This practice continues today and in the same form. Think of the typical American city regulating the number and location of pawnshops, adult bookstores, liquor stores, and more recently cannabis dispensaries. Think of the conditions and limitations imposed on them, such as hours of operation, onsite security, and detailed record-keeping. In today's municipality these conditions are usually monitored by code enforcement. In colonial Boston, we find the *constables* who were from time to time to search throughout the limits of their area "so oft as they shall see cause, for all offenses and offenders against this Law."[36] And if a constable neglected his duty, fines were to be levied on him by the Marshal. This law, passed in 1648 with Boston's population being about two thousand,[37] shows us the already-familiar pattern: a threat to order is identified, a new regulation is passed, and a new enforcer is created.

***

---

[35] Ibid., p. 30.

[36] The Laws and Liberties of Massachusetts, p. 31.

[37] Kennedy, p. 255 Appendix A.

We will return to Boston in another chapter. But now, using the City upon a Hill as an inspiration, let us note that communal order can be utopian. Because it is not an actual state of events but an ideal in which we think we would all like to live, order has the tendency to expand, almost indefinitely. In its expansion, it may become detached from reality and move into ethereal heights. The better actual conditions are—the safer, the cleaner, the quieter our environment—the more time and energy we seem to have to dream about other, even better things. So far, we have encountered only the basic features of order: safety, cleanliness, animal control, and disruptive behavior. In the upcoming chapters, we will see other elements that were deemed desirable to be part of communal order; for example, some pleasing-to-the-eye, aesthetic features of the built environment. Whether such elements of communal order should or should not be enshrined in law has been a question for political communities to answer. Some have and others have not. Our point here is simply that communal order is not a stable concept. It is a constantly moving goalpost, a mirage on the desert's horizon.

It is also a good time to point out the delicate and elusive balance between communal order and personal freedom. Such a balance is difficult to find or even define. We can never be sure how much order we want in our life and how much freedom we are willing to give up for it. Saying "we want order" we often mean that we had rather have orderliness outside ourselves, for orderliness in others makes our life more predictable and safer. But it is not that we would want to have total order outside—we would not want to live inside a machine. Only *some* amount of order is needed. At the same time, we want to retain our own freedom to allow ourselves to pursue what we value. But since we rely on other people to give us what we value, we need to grant them freedom, so they pursue what they value. This means a certain amount of disorder must be accepted. But how much can we tolerate? It is not known. It depends on one's age, location, personal situation, and perhaps the time of the day. In addition, the balance between freedom and order is difficult to find inside ourselves. We would not want to be completely free from any structure because without it we would become unmoored, being tossed about by our own desires like the boats in a storm. So, we need order within us. But not too much of it either, for we are not machines. Something about too much freedom and too much order makes us equally uneasy. But where is the golden mean? We do not know. With so much uncertainty, can we really hope to build a city upon a hill?

7
SAN FRANCISCO GOLD AND CHAOS

*One hundred thousand men from all quarters of the globe
suddenly finding themselves thrown together in a new land,
without established government, and all intent upon the rapid
acquisition of wealth—was ever the stage better set for
a lawless and blood-thirsty drama?*

Owen Cochran Coy

Discussing a community establishing and maintaining order, we should remember that the American settlement of the early seventeenth century was not governed democratically. It would not be accurate to suggest that new dangers to order were perceived by the community as a whole, or that the community as a whole demanded government action that resulted in a new law. This may be happening today, but not then. In the Colonial period, rather than being promulgated through a democratic process, laws and regulations were imposed upon the general population, even when it was small, by the ruling few. In New Amsterdam, for example, it was the energetic Director General Pieter Stuyvesant whose administration passed down most of the new laws; in

Massachusetts Bay, they were forced by what historian Hugh Brogan called the "enlightened despotism" of John Winthrop; and in the 1611 Jamestown, Virginia, it was Governor Thomas Dale's military-like code that brought a harsh version of communal order to the settlers.[38] But the mid-nineteenth century San Francisco was different. When faced with challenges to its law and order, the citizens themselves took the initiative, organized themselves, and acted.

In 1847, San Francisco was a *pueblo* with some 400 residents. Nominally it was under Mexican control and run by an *alcalde* (mayor) and *ayuntamiento* (town council). But its closest Mexican official was more than a hundred miles south, in Monterey, California, and San Francisco was a sleepy town. It lay near a convenient bay, though, and in due time it would have grown, no doubt, through gradual foreign immigration and industrialization, just as like New York, Boston, and other seaports. But *due time* was not meant for San Francisco. The discovery of gold a hundred thirty miles northeast in January of 1848 turned this quiet place into a teeming beehive almost overnight.

At first, though, the rumors of gold found near Sierra Nevada got the town almost depopulated. Residents rushed to the foothills so quickly that most businesses had to suspend their operations. They had neither customers nor employees. By May 1848, three quarters of all men from San Francisco were in the mines. The land values dropped by more than fifty per cent.[39] But as the news of gold found in large quantities had been confirmed and spread throughout California, its neighboring states, and eventually the world, the population began swelling like a tsunami wave. San Francisco harbor became the point of destination for hundreds of vessels bringing human cargo from as far away as South America, Australia, and China. In his book *Gold Days*, Owen Cochran Coy reported that by the middle of 1849 more than six hundred ships

---

[38] On Dale's Code, see Encyclopedia Britannica, 15th Edition, Volume 29, page 204.

[39] Owen Cochran Coy. <u>Gold Days</u>. Los Angeles, Ca: Powell Publishing Company, 1929, p. 60.

had arrived at the San Francisco bay bringing with them some 40,000 people.[40] Those were only from the ports in the Pacific Ocean basin— they could reach the Golden Gate quicker. More vessels, going around the horn of Patagonia, would arrive in the fall. Once in the harbor, ships often could not leave even if their captains had wished them to (and many did not) because immediately upon arrival their sailors ran ashore, just as their passengers, not to be found again. The harbor looked like a "forest of masts," a ghost shipyard filled with forsaken vessels under the multitude of foreign flags. At the same time, thousands of gold seekers, who could not pay the boat fare, were on their way overland towards California from the Midwest and Eastern states.

Most of the new arrivals wasted no time in town but continued towards the American River at the foothills of Sierra Nevada. But many craftsmen and merchants decided to settle in San Francisco, realizing that the miners would soon need goods and services. The result was that by February 1849 San Francisco's population grew to 2,000; by August it was 6,000; and by winter, when the miners returned, 20,000.[41] By July 1850, some 626 vessels lay in the bay and nearby harbors, and the population of San Francisco was 94,766.[42] The city was crowded with hotels, saloons, theaters, and gambling houses, accommodating new arrivals and providing entertainment for weary miners eager to spend their hard-earned wealth. Between April 1849 and April 1850, more than sixty thousand men arrived, and only two thousand women.[43]

A plot of real estate that cost $16 in 1847 sold for about $45,000 a year and a half later. Building supplies were short and labor scarce and expensive (everyone was "gone to the diggings"), so houses were often manufactured elsewhere (as far as in Boston and China) and shipped to

---

[40] Ibid., p. 244.

[41] Ibid., p. 247.

[42] *The Virtual Museum of the City of San Francisco* at www.sfmuseum.org/hist/chron2.html.

[43] *The Virtual Museum of San Francisco* at www.sfmuseum.org/hist/chron2.html.

San Francisco to be assembled on site.[44] All in all, between thirty and one hundred houses were built daily, and the city mushroomed.[45] To meet the demand for buildings, some of the abandoned ships were brought onshore to serve as hotels, and one, still in the harbor, was utilized as a floating jail.[46]

At first there was no attempt to build permanent housing, wrote historian Zoeth Skinner Eldredge, because very few people thought of staying in San Francisco for long. So, "[h]ouses were built of the flimsiest construction, and most of them, when finished at all inside, were lined with cotton cloth in lieu of plaster."[47] Anything that could provide protection against the winds and rains was utilized: a tent, a dry goods box, a hastily constructed shanty lined with bunk beds. One area close to the shore contained about a thousand tents made of cloth.[48] Writer Bayard Taylor, who visited San Francisco in August 1849, described his impression so:

> Hundreds of tents and houses appeared, scattered all over the heights, and along the shore for more than a mile. A furious wind was blowing down through a gap in the hills, filling the streets with clouds of dust. On every side stood buildings of all kinds, begun or half-finished, and the greater part of them were

---

[44] Zoeth Skinner Eldredge. The Beginnings of San Francisco. NY: John C. Rankin Company, 1912, p. 595.

[45] *The Gold Rush: San Francisco* at www.pbs.org gives the number at thirty houses a day while Eldredge writes that "houses sprang up by hundreds overnight" (p. 595).

[46] *California History* by Ralph Berger at www.ccent.com. A remarkable map showing sunken ships and the original shoreline of Yerba Buena can be found on the National Park Service website at https://www.nps.gov/safr/learn/historyculture/buried-ships-of-san-francisco.htm#:~:text=%5B03:05%5D%20ELLIOT:,out%20into%20Yerba%20Buena%20Cove. Search also for San Francisco Maritime and Buried Ships of San Francisco.

[47] Eldredge, p. 594.

[48] Ibid., pp. 592-593.

mere canvas sheds, open in front, and covered with all kinds of signs, in all languages.[49]

The first major fire occurred in December 1849. About fifty houses around the central plaza were destroyed and the loss was estimated at one million dollars. The adjoining blocks were saved only because burning buildings were pulled down quickly enough or covered with wet blankets to minimize the spread.[50] Although the destroyed houses were quickly replaced, within the following two years the town burnt down five more times. On May 4, 1850, for example, a fire engulfed an entire city block bounded by Kearny, Clay, Montgomery and Washington Streets, jumping across Washington Street to the buildings on the other side. One person died, several more were injured by firearms that discharged on their own from the heat, about 300 buildings burnt, causing $4,000,000 in damage.[51]

The streets upon which these tents and houses stood were uneven, unpaved, and almost impassable, especially during the rainy season of 1849-1850. "So deep was the mud," wrote Eldredge, "that horse and wagon were sometimes literally swallowed up in it, while the owner narrowly escaped a similar fate."[52] Needless to say, San Francisco's municipal authorities were not prepared for anything of such magnitude. Although they arranged for brush wood and limbs of trees to be thrown into the streets to stabilize the mud, it helped neither the rider nor the transporter: mules' and horses' legs would routinely become entangled in the sunk brush. It was not uncommon to see a mule stalled in the sludge unable to move with only his head above it, or a rider drowned after his horse's legs became trapped in the brush. The

---

[49] Quoted in Coy, p. 247.
[50] Eldredge, p. 594.
[51] *The Virtual Museum of the City of San Francisco* at http://www.sfmuseum.org/hist/chron2.html.
[52] Ibid., pp. 596-597.

rumor was that in the mire of Montgomery Street one could find human bodies.[53]

When dry, the streets were filled with trash, rubbish, and waste, for there was no organized attempt or municipal service to clean them. Exacerbating the condition was that the influx of goods into the city was speedier than anyone's ability to sell or consume them. The shipments of cargo arrived in San Francisco in numbers far in excess of the demand. Rather than paying for storage, it was often cheaper to abandon them. Muddy sidewalks were often lined with materials whose storage would cost more than their value. According to Eldredge, many "tons of wire sieves, iron, rolls of sheet lead, cement, and barrels of beef were sunk in the mud."[54] Filled with such refuse, the town had become a haven for rats of all colors. Black, brown, gray, of a "monstrous size, fierce, voracious, and destructive," they were seen swimming in the bay, climbing ships, swarming around troughs and ovens, hoarding in kitchens and bedchambers. Walking the streets at night, one could hardly avoid being brought into contact with them.[55]

However disorderly physical San Francisco was, its potential for social disorder was greater. Eldredge described the town as being "full of gamblers, thieves, and cut-throats from every quarter of the globe."[56] Murders were committed daily, everybody was a law unto himself, and by midsummer of 1849 the situation reached its peak. A description from Eldredge's book is worth quoting in full:

> [In early 1849, an] organization, formed from the riffraff of the disbanded regiment of New York volunteers, joined by Australian convicts and the scum of the town, paraded the streets with drum and fife and streaming banners, spreading

---

[53] Eldredge, p. 597.
[54] Ibid., p. 598.
[55] Ibid., p. 596.
[56] Ibid., pp. 598-600.

terror and dismay among the people. They called themselves Hounds or Regulators, and under pretense of watching over public security, intruded themselves in every direction and committed all sorts of outrageous acts. Relying on strength of numbers and arms, they levied forced contributions upon the merchants for the support of their organization. [...] The culmination of their reign was reached when, on the night of July 15, 1849, they made an attack in force upon the Chileno quarter [...] robbing, beating, and seriously wounding the inhabitants and destroying their tents and houses.[57]

Eldredge's description is important because it makes a powerful illustration for our discussion on communal order. It shows that whenever human beings live together, they always seek to organize into some kind of order and establish some kind of rule. The situation described by the historian is remarkable not so much because of the boldness of the gang of thugs, but because they called themselves *regulators*. They formed an *organization*. They proclaimed to be watching over others' *security*. They even levied a *tax*. They saw themselves, not at all unjustifiably, as filling a vacuum. A human settlement cannot exist without order, and the so-called regulators offered one—the only one they could fathom—based on terror. However unjust, it was still an order. Without some form of it, no community can exist. It is common that in the absence of a lawfully maintained order, sooner rather than later an unlawful one will be imposed.

It is a known historical pattern that bad men with arms can only be stopped by good men with arms. Luckily for San Francisco, the response to the challenge by the Regulators was swift. Writing about the life of "forty-niners," Owen Cochran Coy pointed out that while many authors in their descriptions of the Golden Rush dwelled on

---

[57] Eldredge, pp. 598-600.

lawlessness and disorder, yet "the outstanding characteristic [was] rather that there was so much order and business-like activity under such extraordinary conditions." Coy attributed this to the Anglo-American capacity for self-government. Under the 1848 Treaty of Guadalupe Hidalgo, Mexico ceded to the United States what is today the territories of California, New Mexico, Arizona, and Texas. By the time of the Golden Rush, San Francisco had been in the formal possession of the Americans for about a year. It seemed that history offered them a test: Could they help a troubled city to establish communal order? Coy's conclusion that "[i]n California, for the first time, Americans were able to demonstrate their ability to set up a new government in accordance with their own ideals" seems justified.[58]

On February 12, 1849 a town meeting was called on San Francisco's central plaza. Attended by many prominent and ordinary residents, the meeting adopted resolutions to hold the election for a legislative assembly "whose power, duty, and office was to make such laws as they in their wisdom might deem essential to promote the happiness of the people."[59] Within the same year, the town council organized a complete municipal service, including surveyor, tax collector, and treasurer. The newly appointed chief of police was tasked with organizing a police force of thirty men, which was later increased to fifty.[60] The first volunteer fire company formed in June of 1850 and was immediately followed by two more companies. Before the end of the year five other fire and "hook and ladder and hose" companies were organized.[61]

The town authorities acted as swiftly as they could and used their powers to the fullest, but the challenges were great and the residents impatient. Some eagerly organized themselves into spontaneous "vigilance committees" to fill in what they believed were the gaps of

---

[58] Coy, p. 165.
[59] Eldredge, p. 601.
[60] Ibid., p. 606.
[61] Eldredge, pp. 594-596.

enforcement. Vigilance committees formed twice, in 1851 and 1856, promising to act as watchdogs. They did not hesitate to take law into their own hands either. Before they were forced to disband, they hanged four men, captured and handed to the police fifteen more, and whipped and deported twenty-nine.[62]

As for the Regulators, they were dealt with shortly after the attack on the Chileno quarter. Alarmed residents assembled on the central plaza, and two hundred and thirty of them organized themselves into a special police force for defense and public order. Four more companies of volunteers, each consisting of a hundred men, formed shortly after. They were under command of men whose names we now recognize in the streets of San Francisco: McAllister, Ellis, Bluxome, and Spofford. Under their leadership, the newly formed paramilitary police forces entered the gang's headquarters and arrested the leader and nineteen others. The rest of the gang scattered in all directions never to be seen again.[63]

***

Aside from the dramatic events involving public safety, we shall review the more routine rules San Francisco passed to protect communal order. Many of them we recognize as familiar to us from other cities, such as those addressing fire safety and sanitary conditions. For example, one 1853 ordinance provided "for the more perfect Protection of Property from Fire," prohibiting erection of awnings or piazzas, extending over the sidewalks unless they were constructed of iron or metal frames. The same ordinance mandated that the Fire Wardens (today we would call them building or fire inspectors) ensure that every stove pipe or chimney extended at least four feet above the building to which it was attached.

---

[62] Library of Congress at http://memory.loc.gov/ammem/cbhtml/cbgovern.html.
[63] Ibid., pp. 598-600.

Another 1853 ordinance prohibited actions dangerous to public health, addressed the construction of privies and vaults, and empowered the City Marshal to conduct inspections and enforce the ordinance. For the first time in California, this document addressed apartment buildings (called tenements) and sanitary control. Every tenement was to have a bathroom in the basement, its vault being sunk underground at least ten feet deep. The walls were to be of brick or stone and be at least two feet from any property line. All house offal, consisting of animal or vegetable substance, had to be deposited in vessels to be emptied at least three times a week. It was prohibited to throw offal or straw, hay, ashes, soot, glass, glass bottles, crockery-ware, iron, nails, or any article or substance whatever into any public place. All wastewater from private properties had to be conducted, by a covered drain, into the street sewer or gutter. This ordinance was enforced by the building wardens.

In April 1852 regulations, however, we encounter something we did not see before: an *Act Providing for the Erection of a Powder Magazine in San Francisco*. This two-page document passed by the State Assembly was the first law in California addressing what we today would call hazardous materials. Its primary goal was to build a public gunpowder storage so that citizens would not have to keep excessive amounts of powder at home. But it also stipulated the maximum amounts one could keep at home. The amounts were up to five pounds for an ordinary citizen and up to twenty-five pounds if one was a merchant. The rest had to be stored elsewhere. The rule also stipulated the safety conditions for gunpowder storage: "in a strong, iron, or copper chest, well secured and fastened, with the word 'Powder' distinctly painted upon it." The chest was to "be kept within three feet of the main entrance of the place in which said powder is kept, so that, in the event of fire, it may be easily removed." The punishment for non-compliance was from one to five hundred dollars at the discretion of the authorities.[64]

---

[64] *Laws of the State of California*, Third Session, Chapter CXXIX., p. 205.

And in an 1854 ordinance we find another familiar title: health inspectors. "And there shall be nominated [...] three or more citizens, who are willing to act in the capacity of Health Inspectors, without receiving any pay." The familiarity is not limited to the fact that two hundred years earlier New Amsterdam and Boston enforcers were also volunteers. The similarity between them is that none specialized in health-related inspections as we understand them today. They did much more. "It shall be the duty of the Health Inspectors to visit and inspect all places where a nuisance detrimental to health exists, or is by them believed to exist, and to order the abatement or removal thereof, and at their discretion to complain of the same to the Recorder; and they, or either of them, shall have power to forbid the landing of passengers or cargoes, supposed to be infecting or contagious, for twenty-four hours, reporting the same immediately to the Board. [. . .] The said Health Inspectors shall also have power to act as policemen and have the power of Fire Wardens."

San Francisco health inspectors, just as their predecessors, point to a universal trend: no matter what their title is, early enforcers are volunteers and generalists. Only later do they begin being paid and specializing in narrow fields.

***

The City of San Francisco incorporated in April 1850, and in September of that year California was admitted to the Union as a new state. Although city- or statehood did not by themselves bring law and order to San Francisco or California, they brought legal authority to regulate their own affairs. To do so, they did not have to invent anything new. Just as New Amsterdam and Boston colonists had followed the traditional Dutch and Tudor legislation they knew from their home countries, San Francisco used the experience of older American cities. Plenty of it had been accumulated by the mid-19th century. Boston had a paid municipal fire department for fifteen years.[65] New York was a metropolis of more than a half million (excluding Brooklyn) with a well-developed regulatory apparatus.[66] Philadelphia had built its public water works forty years earlier. Baltimore installed street gas lamps by 1816.[67] Buffalo had been regulating its burial business, and Milwaukee had long passed a noise ordinance prohibiting ringing bells and outcries at the markets.[68] San Francisco, when its turn came, stood on their shoulders. It used their experience when laying pipes to bring water to the fire department and installing gas lamps to light the streets. The city's first fire company was headed by a former New York fireman, David Broderick, and its police was organized by a former New York policeman Malachi Fallon.

By 1860, close to twelve hundred million dollars' worth of gold had passed through San Francisco, and its population stabilized at 56,000.[69] The Gold Rush was over. The survival and later flourishing of the city proved that the near-collapse of its nascent days was overcome successfully by the American-style self-government. Communal order was restored and, as it happened in other times and places too, substantially expanded in later years.

---

[65] Arthur M. Schlesinger. "A Panoramic View: The City in American History" in The City in American Life from Colonial Times to the Present. Paul Kramer and Frederick L. Holborn, eds. NY: G.P. Putnam's Sons, 1970, pp. 23-24.

[66] The Bureau of the Census at http://www.census.gov/population/documentation/twps0027/tab08.txt.

[67] Constance McLaughlin Green. The Rise of Urban America. NY: Harper & Row, Publishers, 1965, pp. 77-78.

[68] Bayrd Still. "Patterns of Mid-Nineteenth-Century Urbanization in the Middle West" in The City in American Life from Colonial Times to the Present. Paul Kramer and Frederick L. Holborn, eds. NY: G.P. Putnam's Sons, 1970, pp. 157-158.

[69] Jeremiah F. Sullivan. Seventy-Five Years of Law in California: How Adventurous Gold Miners Won Immortal Fame as Lawmakers. The Virtual Museum of the City of San Francisco at www.sfmuseum.org, accessed on 3-22-05. The Library of Congress's website at http://memory.loc.gov, accessed on 3-15-5.

8

DOES CODE ENFORCEMENT SIGNAL A CULTURAL SHIFT?

Before we move on to consider another city as an example of communal order's expansion, let us review what we have learned so far. We have seen that the first municipal laws and their enforcers appeared in response to threats and challenges: physical deficiencies (such as dirty chimneys and trash) as well as bad behavior (raucous drinking). We saw that the threats were triggered (mostly but not exclusively) by a growing population. We discussed how new laws and regulations led to first enforcers, who were ordinary citizens who volunteered to watch over others. They did not think of themselves as precursors of new occupations. They simply did what they all felt was needed to be done, and the transition from a private citizen to a volunteer enforcer must have been smooth. We noted, too, a potential conflict of interests it entailed. If you are a carriage maker in New Amsterdam, how easy is it to turn into a chimney inspector in your spare time? How aggressively would you force your neighbors to clean their chimneys? You could do this either if you were the *only* carriage maker in town, without competition, or if your reputation was so high that you would not be afraid of losing potential customers. But even then, how comfortable would you be interfering with your neighbor's hearth if your children played together with hers? In a small community, where everyone knew each other, the tendency would have been to dissociate this awkward duty from neighborly relationships. And this is what we observed too. Rather sooner than later, with public finance permitting, a professional enforcer emerged—one without other obligations and without conflicts of interest either.

We also noted that the volunteers' duties were by today's standards generalized, not specialized. Like the old-time physician who treated pneumonia, mended broken bones, pulled teeth, and did surgery, early enforcers regulated whatever was necessary to regulate. The laws were few in numbers and they were commonsensical, so no special knowledge would have been required to administer them. Even later when volunteer fire companies were formed, one did not have to go through training to become a fireman. Any able-bodied male willing to pay for his own tools and uniform could do it. Because of this lack of specialization, even as late as in the 19th century, able-bodied males serving as volunteer firemen were expected to do other things as well. In 1850, for example, some fifty of them from the San Francisco Protection Engine Company were asked to go to Sacramento to put down a riot.[70] That firemen would assist the police in suppressing a riot is almost inconceivable today when each occupation is highly specialized. It was not until the appearance of the steam fire engine, which required training to operate, that firemen began to be employed through public funds and became the professionals they are today.[71]

As we reviewed New Amsterdam, Boston, and San Francisco, we saw that how people define communal order tended to expand, not to contract. The first law related to building construction in California, for example, was a single-page document. The California Tenement House Act of 1909 was fifteen and a half pages long. Today the California Building Code alone has three volumes, some eight hundred pages each, and this is not to mention the Plumbing, Electrical, Mechanical, and other technical codes. This is not unique to California, but a universal trend. As one example, the number of ordinances related to public safety in the cities of Albany and New York between 1707 and 1773 went up from 10 percent to 30 percent of the total number of ordinances.[72] If we assume that how we define communal order is

---

[70] *The Virtual Museum of the City of San Francisco* at www.sfmuseum.org/hist/chron2.html, accessed on 7-15-19.
[71] Still, pp. 165-167.
[72] Eric H. Monkkonen. America Becomes Urban: the development of U.S. cities and towns, 1780-1980. Berkeley and Los Angeles, Ca.: University of California Press, 1988, p. 94.

expressed in new rules we pass, the numerical increase alone tells us that the modern definition of order is larger than before. Why?

One reason, of course, is the perception of disorder that accompanies any population growth. Urban areas feel more disorderly, whether or not they really are. Being surrounded by strangers, coming and going, simply does not make a person feel safer. Objectively too, the anonymity the modern city provides to us all makes for more fertile ground for crime. When rule-breakers cannot be detected as easily as they can escape, it is only natural that urban dwellers feel threatened. They demand more protection. They create more rules. They require more enforcers. And while the police are dealing with serious threats to order, its junior partner can take care of non-serious ones. Clotheslines in front yards, Christmas lights on display in February, fences being a few inches too high are all signs of an enlarged concept of order, and they are the bread and butter of code enforcement.

But there are other reasons too why the modern definition of order is expanding. The sheer size and complexity of modern society seem to require more regulation. It is not because we do not value individual freedom but, paradoxically, because we want more of it. Imagine a glass ball in which particles move around in a sort of Brownian motion. They cross paths, bump into each other, change directions, with larger ones smashing smaller ones out of their ways, and all scattering throughout the ball randomly. This system may seem tolerable if we watch it from the outside. But if we are the particles—some larger, some smaller— moving inside the ball, such a system is not a system, but a chaos. As particles, we care that we should be free to go in the direction we want to go and that nothing bumps us out of our way. This means that we must restrict other particles, large or small, from bumping into us. And in return, we must agree not to bump into them. We must, in other words, establish rules of conduct, and the larger the ball and the more numerous the particles, the more elaborate those rules will be. We want freedom to pursue our direction, and this means we must control our own bumping and that of others.

In a highly complex system, such as our society, there are more rules than ever before. We are subject to them at different levels. When we install a new faucet in the kitchen sink, we are subject to the rules of building code and the homeowner association. When we cross the street, we are subject to state regulation controlling where we can do it. When we take a child to school, we are subject to the rules of the board of education. We pay rent, and we are subject to the rules of the lease. We pay taxes, and we are subject to the tax code. We drive on a highway, and we are subject to the vehicle code. We board a plane, and we are subject to federal regulations. We make a living, and we are subject to rules of the union and the workplace that hires us, and they themselves are subject to rules by the state. This is not to suggest that those rules are not repetitive, overlapping, or contradictory, but only that society as free as ours must, to avoid chaos, develop so many.

Another reason for the number of rules and laws is that we keep passing them in pursuit of an order of our imagination. It is not clear if a cat or a dog imagines a better future, but humans do. In our imagination, order is always better than the one we have. In our imagination it is beautiful and strong (for nothing can harm it there); in real life, it is always somewhat chipped off. When imaginary order materializes in things like streets and houses and human beings, it turns out slightly damaged. Suddenly, it has a myriad of features, big and small, none of which is perfect. Imaginary streets are clean and straight. Actual streets have trash and uneven sidewalks. Order, once materialized, falls into disorder. But we, who yearn for order, keep passing new laws in an attempt to make dreams real. We will, I think, continue doing so, not only because such is human nature, but also because our civilization imagines history as having a direction. It has hopes for a brighter future. To bring it about, it will keep making more rules.

Another preliminary conclusion is that code enforcement performs duties of two different kinds: old and new. I began the book by proposing that code enforcement was a new occupation. Yet throughout the previous chapters I have kept noting how similar the old duties were to the modern ones, only their names were different. The answer to this is that both statements can be true at the same time: code enforcement is indeed relatively new, *and* it has absorbed some of the old duties. Old threats to order are still with us and always will be, and to the degree that code enforcement addresses them, it does what others have done before. The name may be different, but the essence is the same. Yet what is important to note is that in addition to the old duties, it is also enforcing something that was not enforced before—issues of purely "cosmetic" nature. In this respect, code enforcement's emergence may be seen as a symptom—or to say it more charitably a symbol—of some qualitative change, some cultural shift.

Has there been a shift—a shift from understanding order as basic to understanding order as more refined? It remains to be seen. But if it is true that there has been such a shift, this would be important for us to notice. And if I claim that code enforcement is, somehow, a symptom of it, this would be important too, if true. I hope not to be assigning to my beloved occupation too much undue importance, but let us follow where evidence and observation take us. Assuming for a moment that this is true, the next question to be asked is this: What do we mean by cosmetic and is it necessarily bad (superficial, unimportant) that society strives for it? What if society indeed develops a new thirst for the fine and delicate and therefore becomes less tolerant of the ugly? What if society translates this intolerance into a government mandate to fight ugliness?

If we assume that the shift is real, this will indicate an affluent and refined culture. There would be nothing new about it. The greatest works of Western art, literature, and architecture have been produced by affluent and refined cultures such as Ancient Athens, Imperial

Rome, or Renaissance Florence. And one may argue, of course, that such works were cosmetic too, because they were not concerned with the issues of physical survival, of life and death. Indeed, not having an architectural gem in your town or a Renaissance painting in your local museum does not make one go hungry; it does not endanger anyone's life or limb. Yet, great works of art are concerned with something that is no less important for man—the spirit, the creativity, the love for truth, beauty, and goodness. And if our ability to appreciate beauty, among other things, is what distinguishes us from animals, this is not at all unimportant. And if affluent societies—commercial republics such as ours—have the means and leisure to allow artistic talent to develop thrive, what could be wrong with that? And if code enforcement is somehow a reflection of this elevated sophistication and refinement in society, perhaps it should console or even congratulate itself for being part of something as important as protecting physical health and safety.

But it is one thing to value art and culture and quite another to ask your local government to instill them as a matter of law. What seems indisputable, at any rate, is that in addition to the old threats to order, code enforcement does address new ones—some quite cosmetic—and it may well be due to the fact that society, for better or for worse, is more sensitive to them now than it was ever before. Preoccupied with smaller and smaller irritants, petty and superficial as they may be, it gives birth, sooner or later, to something akin to fashion police.

In the following chapter, we will consider the city of Philadelphia as an example showing how organically the notion of communal order grows and expands to include the beautiful and pleasing on a public scale.

9
PHILADELPHIA FOUNTAINS

Philadelphia was devastated by yellow fever twice: in 1793 and 1798. In his book *The Sanitary City*, Martin Melosi explained that the late eighteenth century understanding of what caused epidemics was rather vague. The city fathers suspected, however, that the cause must have been either bad air or, more likely, bad water. If it was water, it must have been polluted in the wells or in the underground cisterns. Something needed to be done. The old water systems needed to be replaced by something safer, a sanitary, city-wide water supply.[73]

In 1801, the first public water-works in the United States was completed in Philadelphia. It was meant to solve more than one problem. First, it provided fresh water for drinking and washing. Second, the water could be used for cleaning the streets from ashes, refuse, and animal manure more easily. Third, it ensured adequate supply and ready access to water for fire protection. Before the water-works it would take fifteen minutes for the bucket brigade to fill up a fire engine; the new system did it within a minute and a half. Fourth, the water-works also included a novelty important for our analysis of communal order: several public fountains.[74]

---

[73] Martin V. Melosi. <u>The Sanitary City: urban infrastructure in America from colonial times to the present.</u> Baltimore, Maryland: The Johns Hopkins University Press, 2000, p. 30. The 1805 *Scott's Geographical Dictionary*, quoted by Melosi, describes the condition of water in Philadelphia as being "so corrupt by the multitude of sinks and other receptacles of impurity, as to be almost unfit to be drank" [sic].

[74] Melosi, p. 27.

We should not miss the significance of this last innovation. It lies in the fact that a useful and practically necessary water system brought about something *in addition* to its practical usefulness, something that had only *aesthetic* value. For in terms of practicality, a public fountain is useless. It could not protect the city against fires or disease; its water could not be drunk. Yet, in the minds of Philadelphia city fathers it was a desirable thing, and worth the expense. Why? Because of man's need, whenever he can, to beautify his environment. Philadelphians were no exception to this need.

Discussing what constitutes orderly life, we may note that in planning a new water system, Philadelphians expanded their view of communal order. An orderly Philadelphia in their vision would have clean streets, healthy and well-washed residents, plenty of water to put out a fire, *and* a few fountains to please the eye. The definition of communal order was now expanded to include an element of beauty.

Another principle in the Philadelphia fountains deserves mention. It is related to how enforcement duties expand. The principle may be called "expansion by convenience." Consider an example. Let us say, we live in Los Angeles but have been given tickets to hear a great opera singer in San Francisco. So, we drive north some 380 miles to go to the opera house. But once we are in San Francisco, we say to ourselves "We are here already, why not go to Alcatraz tomorrow?" Because we have committed so much time and effort already, other options suddenly become available. We can even formulate the common-sense principle in something sounding a bit more scientific: *When an expenditure of energy occurs in order to achieve a goal, other goals become feasible because of their closeness in time and space.* The Philadelphia authorities must have gone through this kind of reasoning when they decided for the fountains to be. We are already investing so much money, why not spend a little more and beautify the city with fountains?

I remind the reader of this natural way of thinking because the expansion by convenience is how we do things every day, and the early enforcers did too. Their duties expanded naturally and organically because of closeness in time and space.[75] For this is what we call convenient: closeness either in time or in space, or both. Initially, the watchmen in the towns surrounding Massachusetts Bay were simply to "walk the rounds in and about the streets, wharves, lanes, and principal inhabited parts [...] to prevent any danger by fire, and to see that good order is kept, taking observation and inspection of all houses and families of evil fame," wrote historian Roger Lane. But in Boston, yet one further duty was added after a while. The head of the night watch acquired a new title: superintendent of lamps.[76] Who else could light them if not the watchman already there at night?

Philadelphia was the first city to build a public water-works. Before the Civil War, however, other cities quickly joined in, and over one hundred municipal water systems had been built. New technology, such as iron piping, allowed for this as well as other improvements. In 1822, Boston inaugurated gas lighting, and in the following year its first-in-the country public sewerage system.[77] These additions to communal order—good water, indoor plumbing, and well-lit streets—were soon accompanied by expanded enforcement. In the following chapter, we will return to Boston to see how it happened and to meet the man in charge.

---

[75] This is how police officers, as remarked by James Q. Wilson, perform expanded services that may be valuable to the community but unrelated to their main function. "The 'service' functions of the police—first aid, rescuing cats, helping ladies, and the like—are omitted [. . .] because, unlike the law enforcement functions, they are intended to please the client and no one else. [...] It is only a matter of historical accident and community convenience that they are provided by the police." James Q. Wilson. Varieties of Police Behavior: The Management of Law and Order in Eight Communities. Cambridge, Mass.: Harvard University Press, 1968, p. 4.
[76] Lane, p. 11.
[77] Schlesinger, p. 23.

10
19ᵗʜ-Century's Boon and Boston Enforcer

The result was a new concept of orderly city life,
one that no longer rested on a corporate organization of
households, but instead depended upon a complex and
impersonal arrangement of individuals.

Oscar Handlin

The American colonies were established initially for agriculture and trade and populated by tradesmen or farmers. Their location on the Atlantic seaboard rapidly made them into vibrant urban hubs and the ports of call for bustling activities in shipment and migration. Add to the location factor the technological innovations in agriculture that allowed fewer people to work the land—the farmers could feed themselves *and* thousands of city dwellers who did not produce food—and it becomes clear why in addition to New York, Boston, Philadelphia, and Charleston, there also grew cities on the main rivers—Pittsburgh, Cincinnati, Louisville, Nashville, St. Louis—and their sister cities on the Midwest Lakes. Playing important economic roles in their regions, the cities near waterways had jobs, attracting migrants from both interior and abroad. By 1870 the five lake cities (Buffalo, Cleveland, Detroit, Chicago, and Milwaukee) had a combined population 16 times bigger than thirty years earlier, while the population of their respective states only tripled.[78]

---

[78] Still, p. 155.

The table below, compiled from the Bureau of the Census's data, shows a relatively gradual growth of the population in Philadelphia and Boston, but a dramatic growth—almost tenfold—of the population in Baltimore and New York. This took place within fifty years.

Urban Population 1790-1840[79]

City / Year	1790	1800	1810	1820	1830	1840
Philadelphia	28,522	41,220	53,722	63,802	80,462	93,665
Boston	18,320	24,937	33,787	43,298	61,392	93,383
Baltimore	13,503	26,514	46,555	62,738	80,620	102,313
New York	33,131	60,515	96,373	123,706	202,598	312,710

In addition to their dominant role as centers of transportation and distribution, major economic activities were brought to the cities with the advance of the Industrial Revolution. The invention and proliferation of the spinning machine changed the way the manufacturing of clothing had been done, which led in turn to the emergence of factories. The development of the steam engine gave birth to a more efficient way of manufacturing goods; it also revolutionized the way they were transported, first by the steamboat and later by the railway. The new inventions stimulated the economy in the entire nation, but the gravitational forces ran towards the cities, along the lines of the waterways and railroads. With the accumulation of wealth, cities were becoming centers of the emerging banking system and vied among themselves for being the seats of government. Religious, cultural, and educational institutions followed. Thousands of people residing in the cities created ready markets for trades, services, and crafts as well as for the development of arts, music, and theater. Cities began acquiring the economic power and symbolic significance that continue to attract to this day. Within a hundred years, between 1790 and 1890, the

---

[79] The Bureau of the Census at
http://www.census.gov/population/documentation/twps0027/tab02.txt.

population of the United States increased dramatically but unevenly: it concentrated disproportionately in urban areas. While the country's general population grew 16 times, its urban population grew 139 times.[80]

Size matters. Quantitative changes bring about qualitative changes. As the epigraphs for this chapter, I used a great quote from a historian that captures the challenge American cities faced during these hundred years. To unpack the quote from historian Oscar Handlin, he tells us that rather than being part of a household or a guild where man was linked to a network of relationships, hierarchies, and mutual obligations, man of the 19th century became a social unit by himself.[81] The 19th century was not the first time in human history that this happened, but during that century the pattern intensified and became the new norm. Technological innovations changed the traditional character of the American economy; its main drivers were no longer household-based businesses and farms. The American economy was turning to capital and machines. This turn had profound social effects. With the weakening of home-based methods of production there weakened the traditional ways of controlling personal behavior. Man could now leave the family and, if he chose to, completely detach himself from the context in which he grew up. Away from the farm or workshop of his father, he could go to the city to become a factory worker. This is what the historian tells us.

But history is not our only instructor. The laws of physics seem to reinforce the difficulties of maintaining order—not merely in growing space but in advancing time. Physicist Stephen Hawking provides us with an illuminating insight that in a closed system disorder inevitably

---

[80] Schlesinger, p. 29.

[81] Oscar Handlin, "The Modern City as a Field of Historical Study" in <u>The Historian and the City</u>, Oscar Handlin and John Burchard, eds. Cambridge, Mass.: The M.I.T. Press, 1963, p. 9.

increases over time.[82] Not order, but disorder. If we now imagine the city as a closed system, the second law of thermodynamics will be true in a social system no less than in a physical one. In such a system order is so fragile because disorder is more probable.

Surely, no one living in a city today needs deep knowledge of physics to know how disorderly it can be. As was pointed out earlier, no one can fail to notice that an increased number of people creates a more complex social organism with a considerably higher number of variables and variations, and its complexity increases the likelihood of something going wrong. More people living in close proximity to each other means a higher probability of disorderly elements occurring among them. The chain is only as strong as its weakest link. The stability of a community is at the mercy of its most unstable member. In a village, a member can be easily identified and disciplined, or, if that doesn't work, expelled. In a large city where residents cannot unite as readily and where anonymity easily covers mischief, the unstable member moves around freely and migrates from one part to another, unmolested and un-expelled. Detection of crime becomes more difficult too, and the scarce resources are directed towards most serious offenders, which means mere mischief remains unpunished. The preservation of order in a large city, in other words, is at the will of its most disorderly character. Whether this is true mathematically, it is perceived to be so by those living in a city today, and our 18th- and 19th-century forebears were no different. They, who saw increasing numbers of strangers around them, perceived that the potential for disorder was frighteningly high.

---

[82] "[The second law of thermodynamics] says that in any closed system disorder, or entropy, always increases with time. In other words, it is a form of Murphy's law: things always tend to go wrong! An intact cup on the table is a state of high order, but a broken cup on the floor is a disordered state. One can go readily from the cup on the table in the past to the broken cup on the floor in the future, but not the other way around." Stephen Hawking, A Brief History of Time, NY: Bantam Books, 1998, p. 149.

Contributing to the perception was the influx of immigrants speaking foreign languages and practicing strange customs. Many of the north-German immigrants who came in the early 19th century, wrote historian Constance McLaughlin Green, were farmers and upon arrival went straight to the countryside. But those who came later tended to stay in the cities, especially if they were poor, speaking the only language they knew, German. At the same time, most of the canals and the railway roadbeds were worked by Irish immigrants, stirring up uneasiness in Boston and New York that the "alien Roman Catholics," many of whom spoke a heavy brogue and could neither write nor read, would overwhelm those who by that time already considered themselves native Americans. The influx grew even more after the 1847 potato famine in Ireland when a fresh wave of unskilled laborers arrived with their families to the East Coast.[83]

The promise of economic opportunity was one of the city attractions. But the pursuit of opportunity, broadly speaking, requires a special personality. Pursuit of opportunity is different from the skills one develops by tilling the soil season after season or by patiently learning a craft as an apprentice. Pursuit of opportunity calls for a quick thinker and hustler, moving around unattached to anything. The city tended to propel and reward this new type of personality, Oscar Handlin wrote, an entrepreneur for whom the pursuit of individual profit was more important than status in a community. The city now "housed a pack of people seeking after gain."[84]

Of course, one needs to be careful not to generalize too much about city life. It was not a jungle. The new form of organized work—the

---

[83] Constance McLaughlin Green. <u>The Rise of Urban America</u>. NY: Harper & Row Publishers, 1965, p. 76.

[84] Oscar Handlin. "The Modern City as a Field of Historical Study" in <u>The Historian and the City</u>. Oscar Handlin and John Burchard, eds. Cambridge, Mass.: The M.I.T. Press, 1963, p. 9.

factory—required in men a new kind of restraint too. Expected to show up for work on time and be in a condition to work every morning (that is, not too hungover), a factory worker had to develop self-discipline and personal responsibility. Many were able to adjust to this new environment and even prosper in it. But we are discussing communal order here—how it is maintained or threatened—and for the purposes of this discussion the misfit is more consequential than the conformist. For order, as was just suggested, is fragile; it slides into disorder easily, almost by default, and it is the weakest link in the chain that matters, not the strongest.

With the increased population came challenges to the physical environment as well. As the factories hired more workers, mostly immigrants, more housing needed to be built for them quickly and cheaply and more trash to be disposed of. The need for factory housing produced the infamous tenement house which made the old threat of conflagration more urgent. The old system of suppressing fire by the bucket brigade proved utterly ineffective when entire blocks were about to go up in flames. At the same time ravaging epidemics, working in less visible and thus more dangerous ways, threatened to affect areas far beyond the workers' quarters. Epidemics could spill into the more affluent areas of the city.

***

It is small wonder that by now residents perceived cities as dangerous places where people were strangers to each other. The traditional restraints—family, clan, or guild—were no longer available to control personal behavior, and it was necessary for some other, external force to do that. Who else but the local government could provide such a force? Writing about Boston in the early 19th century, historian Roger Lane noted the expansion of basic police functions such as patrol and inspection. "Rootless visitors and residents freed from the old restraints required new and sometimes harsh methods of control."[85] The tasks expected from the government became larger and more complex.

In a way, Boston presented a special case among cities because its physical growth was restrained by its location on a peninsula. The spatially close cohabitation of the wealthy and the poor made social tensions more pulpable. Lane wrote that Boston residents were especially sensitive to unruly conduct. They complained about public peace more often because neighborhoods were not clearly separated, and it was no longer possible to ignore or isolate those areas of the city where disorder and vice prevailed. One of the worst areas was just behind Beacon Hills. Leading citizens of the increasingly fashionable West End complained that they witnessed unpleasant scenes while passing the Common. Two-thirds of all criminal convictions in Boston were obtained in the categories of vagabondage, lewd and lascivious behavior, assault and battery, and common drunkenness.[86]

Old forms of municipal government did not seem adequate for the burgeoning city. For a long time, Bostonians had held town meetings where townspeople gathered to hear their leaders make important decisions. In the mid-18th century, the attendance could be somewhere between 250 and 400. But by the 1780s, wrote Lane, that system no longer worked. In some cases, neither community leaders nor townspeople showed up for the meetings; the town had spread so much that long distances made it difficult for people to gather. But in other cases when especially controversial matters were discussed, large shouting crowds made meetings almost impossible to conduct. As is often the case with easily identifiable minorities, local leaders complained that it was immigrants who weakened the former sense of community. In 1799, to restore intimacy, the large town meeting was entirely bypassed. Instead, officers representing their wards were now

---

[85] Lane, p. 2.
[86] Ibid., p. 6.

elected and sent to the meetings.[87] To be run efficiently, an enterprise—be it a community, an organization, or a meeting—its members should be able to recognize each other's faces. We can see in this an example how size, when it reaches a certain point, makes effective running of the community difficult. And when it becomes large enough, it begins breaking into smaller and more manageable parts.

***

The career of Benjamin Pollard, Boston's City Marshal between 1823 and 1836, allows us to see how the newly incorporated city with the challenges to its order. His career is a real-life example of the features outlined earlier: the broad variety of duties, the initial expansion by convenience, the following specialization and subdivision into smaller units, the vagueness of the legal language, and the maintenance of order. Pollard wore, as the saying goes, multiple hats, handling duties that today constitute separate occupations. He was the first marshal of the city, but also a health officer. The Council decreed that the department of internal police also be placed under his superintendence. The department was not limited to what we call police today, but handled the care of the streets, common sewers, vaults, and anything else that affected the health, security, and comfort of the city. But the ordinance's language, wrote Lane, provided only general outlines of a code of health, and Pollard had to fill those outlines using common sense and the advice of a group of physicians.

It is useful to see Pollard's duties in light of today's occupations (in parentheses). He reviewed and approved all plans for the disposal of wastewater outside the sewers (plan checker and environmental inspector); process permits for vault emptying (permit technician). Pollard and his staff could enter any house, between sunrise and sunset, to address a nuisance (code enforcement officer or building inspector)

---

[87] Roger Lane. <u>Policing the City: Boston, 1822-1885.</u> Cambridge, Mass.: Harvard University Press, 1967, p. 4.

or, under certain circumstances, arrest people (the police). Since his colleague the city prosecutor handled only the most important cases, Pollard would prosecute minor ones that he chose to bring to court (code enforcement officer when he goes to an administrative hearing).[88]

Pollard supervised the constables on city duty, his own deputies, and independent contractors, teamsters and cartmen, whom he employed to remove dirt from the streets. At the outset his authority was under review by the council, but "by the later 1820s the phrase 'referred to the city marshal' had become the stock answer to most health questions raised in the board of aldermen." Lane explains that the Marshal's office was utilized for an "even greater variety of purposes when growth presented the city with new problems for which there were no traditional solutions." Because the city's administrative machinery was obsolete and bound by long tradition, "the flexibility of the marshal's office was especially useful."[89] The variety of problems and especially the flexibility of the office are quite telling. If we had to choose defining characteristics of today's code enforcement, we would use the same words: variety of problems and flexibility.

When it became necessary to begin licensing dogs in 1825 (animal control) or forbid the use of firearms within city limits (police), the Marshal was asked to do both. He was also charged with shooting stray dogs (animal control) and arresting poachers on the Common (park ranger). To stop looting and disorder during fires, the Marshal was asked to provide oversight (police). He helped to plan processions in public streets and parks (special events coordinator) and assisted the clerks of the markets to maintain peace and order. He reported to the council on issues of new construction (building official). The generalized nature of his duties, Lane writes, allowed him to perform traditional functions formerly exercised by volunteer councilmembers

---

[88] Lane, p. 17.
[89] Ibid., p. 18.

and, in addition, new ones "for which no other machinery had been as yet devised."[90]

In 1839, when in reaction to the proliferation of secondhand dealers and pawn shops, an ordinance was passed that required their licensing, someone had to specialize in its enforcement. Conditions imposed by the ordinance were strict and detailed: the dealers were to record the dates and hours of all transactions along with the names and addresses of the sellers; they were prohibited from buying articles from minors and from operating at irregular hours. To implement the elaborate provisions a special officer position was created in the department.[91]

I examine Pollard's multiple tasks in such detail because they illustrate features and dynamics that are typical of local governments and their enforcement efforts. First, the sheer variety of his duties resembles the variety of code enforcement duties today. Like Pollard, code enforcement officers are expected to be problem solvers and exercise flexibility. The flexibility seems to be baked in the law itself. Like Pollard, who dealt with only "outlines of a code of health," code enforcement, it is worth repeating, works with code language that is more general than specific. The generality of the language provides flexibility to enforce whatever needs to be enforced at the moment. Even when the issue at hand is not spelled out precisely in the law, it can always be fitted under a general, catch-all provision. Another consequence of language's generality is that it allows for limitless expansions by convenience. Finally, just as for Pollard, the generality of the language gives the enforcing officer discretion. He is free to decide what fits and what doesn't into the law; he may give a warning or a citation; he may accept full or less-than-full compliance. Pollard too, as Lane reported, was "proud of the fact that he had seldom to resort to prosecution. Informal warnings, followed if necessary by official notice,

---

[90] Lane, p. 18.
[91] Lane, p. 54.

were ordinarily enough."[92]

Second, as Pollard's duties grew and expanded, within their broad scope formed specialized areas and some of them broke away. Expansion, specialization, and breaking apart took place at the same time. By 1824, Pollard's was already the third department in Boston to exercise police powers (two others were concerned with public order and the regulation of the interment of the dead.[93]). But among all the multiple matters just listed, his focus continued to be sanitation. Polard was not the first in this area of enforcement either. A Board of Health had been created in 1799 after yellow fever struck the city (as it did Philadelphia). It improved the execution of older regulations and developed new ones; during its watch smallpox was eventually brought under control; it administered vessel quarantine and paved the way for new standards for "the cleanliness of cellars, yards, and privies, as well as for the public streets and markets."[94] In continuing the work of the Board of Health, Pollard was, in today's terms, a narrowly specialized health officer. But to perform certain duties well it would no longer be possible to be amateur and carry them out in addition to others. Some duties required dedicated time and expertise. In 1837, for example, the marshal's office lost one of its sanitary functions when the care of the sewer system was moved to a different department where the expertise was.[95]

The 19th-century industrial boom challenged the city's ability to maintain order, requiring integration, specialization, and subdivision. The challenge was nowhere more acute than in handling the tenement, the subject of our next chapter.

---

[92] Lane, p. 18.

[93] Lane, p. 4.

[94] Lane, p. 5. Similarly, in 1804 in New York there was established the first office dealing specifically with sanitation problems. It was called the office of city inspector, and its responsibility was to gather information about public nuisances and report violations to the city council (Melosi, pp. 20-21).

[95] Lane, p. 52.

11
19TH-CENTURY'S BANE AND TENEMENT

A rapidly expanding, heterogeneous, urban-industrial society posed problems of control—physical and social—which overwhelmed its citizens. They had to learn, through experience, which of the multitudinous specialized activities of an urban community could be left entirely in private hands, which required government monopoly, which needed government regulation, and finally, how to organize the system of government services and controls most efficiently.

Roy Lubove

Throughout the nineteenth century city growth intensified. The fact that urban problems had by the time acquired some familiarity did not soften their intensity. The city physiognomy seemed intensely more uneven—black and white with deepening shadows in between. On the bright side, urban life was gleaming and dazzling, boasting the newest technological innovations, highest cultural achievements, and acquisition of great fortunes. It fascinated the minds of contemporaries. Returning, after an absence, to New York in 1870, the great American poet Walt Whitman praised the "splendor, picturesqueness, and oceanic amplitude and rush of these great cities." The poet compared the magnificent work of nature—its mountains, forests, and seas—to the work of man and found them equally great. The streets, goods, houses, ships, and electrifying energy of the crowds of people—no wonder young men and women could not resist the city's magnetic power. "We cannot all live in cities," wrote another writer in 1867, "yet nearly all seem determined to do so."[96]

New beliefs in progress and the power of reason planted in eighteenth century Europe were now blooming in America. The scientific mind would, it seemed, be able to solve the human predicament in the same way it had solved so many other problems. It replaced the muscle with the machine, ushered in the mass production of clothing and food so that famine and cold were no longer feared, increased the speed of transportation, harnessed the wild nature of steam, gas, and electricity. The scientific mind seemed all-powerful, the progress unstoppable, and the city was their materialization and symbol.

On the dark side, urban life displayed smoggy factories, filthy streets, foul back alleys, deafening railroads, abject poverty of so many of its residents, child labor, orphan asylums and poorhouses, prostitution, and—perhaps less noticeable but no less devastating—frustrated hopes.

The economic disparity growing between classes of citizens must have troubled the mind on more than merely economic level. The uneven distribution of wealth seemed to occur in a haphazard manner. Perhaps, in the long term the emerging capitalism rewarded the best, the brightest, and the most industrious, but who had the luxury to wait the long term? Who had the vantage point to see if it was true? Within a short human life, the burgeoning economic system seemed troubling, for far too often economic success went to the most unscrupulous. More importantly, there seemed to be no system, no conventional order in which success followed. The old European layers of the ruling nobility, the bourgeoisie, and the "unwashed masses" might have been

---

[96] Both quotes and analysis are in Schlesinger, p. 28.

unfair but at least it was comprehensible. If you were an heir to a title or land, you would get it; if you were born poor, you would most likely die poor too. At least, it was an *orderly* system; it was not haphazard; it was predictable. The American city in the 19th century offered no such comfort. Success could be, it seemed, won randomly. Rather than being passed from father to son, it rewarded the individual talent and innovative ideas—and those traits could appear randomly in anyone. Where you came from or who your parents were mattered less than what you as an individual were able to do. Providing no sense of order, the city was like an immense casino where anyone could pull the winning lottery ticket. That both success and misery could spring from the same neighborhood kindled imagination on one hand and envy on the other. For some, the city was the gambling house where they could turn an ambition into wealth. For many, the city was the place of forsaken hopes and unfulfilled expectations.

The epicenter of despair and the ugliest feature of urban life, especially after the Civil War, was the tenement house. Tenement was the precursor of a modern apartment building, with many small units along common hallways and only a few common restrooms and washrooms. All the troubling aspects of city life, all the threats to order—crime, vice, fire, and epidemics—seemed to find their embodiment there. Tenement houses, the creatures of industrialization and urbanization, were either built or converted from old stock very quickly to accommodate thousands of people employed by factories and plants— mostly unskilled laborers and their families. A great majority of them were foreign immigrants who arrived at the city by boat and settled there, gladly taking any employment and housing available to them. But the supply into the workforce outweighed the demand, and that led to ruthless conditions both at work and home. Constance McLaughlin Green wrote in her book *The Rise of Urban America* that "[m]achine shop operators, steel workers, and textile mill hands all too often became labor, a commodity to be handled like raw materials, bought as cheaply as the supply permitted and replaced when the purchase price threatened to cut in upon profits. And the ever-renewing throng of European immigrants guaranteed replacements."[97]

Without an economic incentive for improvement and without laws forcing them to improve, the property owners kept housing accommodations to a minimum. Rooms they rented were often without windows, heating facilities, or running water. Pressured by economic necessity, renters often exacerbated their own conditions by subletting a room or a corner of a room to another family, causing severe overcrowding. Concerns over human congestion in tenements were raised, especially by physicians, as early as in the 1820s. But what they had reported then paled in comparison with the conditions in the mid- and late 1800s. This was when more immigrants arrived at the industrial centers. In Chicago, for example, during the years between 1850 and 1860, nearly 50% of the increase in population was by foreign immigration; another similar increase took place between 1860 and 1870.[98] The cities could hardly cope with the swelling population. In New York the favored method of accommodating swarms of newly arrived people was to subdivide large rooms in the downtown old mansions. The mansions became available after their rich owners abandoned them and moved to more fashionable and quieter places. By the mid-19th century even warehouses had been converted into tenements where as many as five or six families could be jammed into a 12-by-14-foot room.[99]

The most vocal reports about dangerous conditions in the tenement came from physicians. They were the only members of the middle class who had to visit the tenement almost daily to treat patients. They saw the conditions with their own eyes. And they were the only professionals whose education and social standing gave weight to their

---

[97] Green, p. 102.

[98] Harvey Warren Zorbaugh. <u>The Gold Coast and the Slum: A Sociological Study of Chicago's Near North Side</u>. The University of Chicago Press, 1929, p. 18.

[99] Green, p. 77.

testimony. Charles Rosenberg in his book *Explaining Epidemics and Other Studies in the History of Medicine* wrote about one such physician, Doctor William Thoms, who published, in 1866, an alarming report. He described one alley where an unusual number of typhus cases had been reported. Visiting an attic room, with a slanted ceiling, measuring only 14 x 7 ½ x 7 feet, the doctor found twelve people. Five of them had typhus. There was no real furniture, and the inhabitants slept on wooden pallets arranged on the floor. One time the doctor found all the children lying naked together (their clothes being washed at the time) on the same mattress and under the same blanket, even though several of them had active cases of typhus. The attic room was so crowded that sometimes the doctor could not make his way to his patients in the corner.[100]

The problem of overcrowding in New York, Philadelphia, Boston, Baltimore, and other cities would not be abated throughout the nineteenth century and even in the first decades of the twentieth. And this was despite many good-faith efforts undertaken by charitable organizations and the enforcement actions attempted by the authorities. According to a report made to the First National Housing Conference in 1911, for example, the Boston health officials took into court a single woman, who lived in an apartment with three small rooms that she sublet to 16 adult lodgers. In another case they found a child, who was reported absent from school, at home sick with scarlet fever. The child lay in bed in the same room with her father, mother, and four brothers and sisters, while four more men slept in the second room and six more in the third.[101]

---

[100] Charles E. Rosenberg. <u>Explaining Epidemics and Other Studies in the History of Medicine</u>. Cambridge University Press, 1992, p. 139.
[101] <u>National Housing Association: Proceedings of the First National Housing Conference held in New York, June 3, 5, and 6, 1911</u>. Proceedings of the Academy of Political Science in the City of New York. New York: The Academy of Political Science, Columbia University, 1912, p. 79.

Needless to say, the residents of tenements suffered from epidemics in disproportionate numbers. Roy Lubove in his book *The Progressives and the Slums* wrote that New York was struck by cholera epidemics in the 1830s and again in the 1840s, and that it "raged most fiercely in the crowded tenement districts, where such scourges as typhoid and typhus fever, pulmonary and diarrheal diseases were also common."[102] But epidemics did not respect class boundaries. The fear of them spreading and affecting indiscriminately the poor and the rich was a driving force among physicians and other conscientious citizens to try to eradicate tenement overcrowding.

The contagious disease was only one of many problems threatening communal well-being. Equally troubling was the fear of the tenement house as a nest of crime, a hot-bed of vice, a breeding ground of dangerous ideas, all of which, if not contained, would infect and destroy the entire city. The memories of the gruesome years of the French Revolution, the emerging theories of socialism, the rising labor movement were on the minds of many a city dweller. They were suspected to have found a welcome home and fertile soil in the tenement crammed with European immigrants. It housed all the elements undermining American values, it was believed to be fraught with moral corrosion. In the words of an 1856 report by a New York State committee that investigated slum conditions in New York, "we must, as a people, act upon this foreign element, or it will act upon us. Like the vast Atlantic, we must decompose and cleanse the impurities which rush into our midst, or [. . .] we shall receive their poison into our whole national system."[103]

The tenement conditions were seen as a failure of social control, wrote Roy Lubove. The slum was not merely a problem of poverty or sanitation. Moral integrity and the communal unity itself were at stake.

---

[102] Roy Lubove, <u>The Progressives And The Slums: Tenement House Reform in New York City, 1890-1917</u>. University of Pittsburgh Press, 1962, p. 11.
[103] Quoted in Lubove, p. 10.

They were threatened by the aliens living in the tenement, who were ignorant of American ways, dirty and diseased, whose thieving, whoring, and drinking threatened to disrupt order and stability. The view of the social reformers was that by improving the housing conditions, they would help transmit to the immigrants the culture and mores of the middle-class.[104]

Without American culture and mores, the tenement dwellers struck fear in the respectable parts of the city. They proved the fears justified too. Their inclination to violence was on display when during the Civil War, in 1863, many of the New York poor came out to protest what they viewed as a discriminatory military draft, streaming "from their gloomy haunts to burn, murder, and pillage." It was because of this threat that in 1860s' New York, for the first time the sanitary and housing reformers were not alone. They found a sympathetic ear and eager support in the perturbed middle class that feared that the immigrant's social and moral state could no longer be ignored.[105]

The contrast between city glamor and tenement misery co-existing so close to each other troubled the scientific mind. How could it be that the pride of Western civilization, its great cities, had been permitted to become "great sores, . . . excrescences upon the body of created things?"[106] The middle of the century, interrupted for several years by the Civil War, saw a number of legislative and administrative attempts to keep the tenement house under control. New York epitomized both the problem and the search for solutions. In 1856, the State Assembly appointed a select committee whose job was to investigate tenement houses in New York and Brooklyn. Several months later it issued a report condemning the capitalist "avarice," the public "lethargy," and

---

[104] Lubove, pp. 10-11.

[105] Lubove, pp. 11-12.

[106] From the 1856 report of the New York State Tenant House Committee, which investigated slum conditions in Brooklyn and New York, quoted in Green, pp. 77-78.

the city's negligence: "Had the evils which now appall us, been prevented or checked in their earlier manifestation, by wise and simple laws, the city of New York would now exhibit more gratifying bills of health, more general social comfort and prosperity, and less, far less expenditure for the support of pauperism and crime."[107] Wise and simple laws were needed urgently.

New York had health inspectors as early as 1804, but by the mid-century they were perceived as highly ineffective. In 1864, a year after the New York riots and while their memory was still fresh, a group of activists called the Council of Hygiene inaugurated a public campaign to improve housing and sanitary standards. When in 1866 a threat of cholera was detected in New York again, another group of resolute physicians took a similar action. They sought to force the city to accept its responsibility to supervise tenements and modernize municipal health services. Using the threat of cholera to agitate public opinion, these groups succeeded in forcing New York to create a new Metropolitan Board of Health.[108] The Board's authority to regulate tenement conditions was embodied in the 1867 New York Tenement House Law.[109]

In addition to the calls for more regulation, there sounded calls for more specialization. Lubove reported that New York's physicians were not only aware of the connection between environment and individual health; they viewed public health as a *specialized* responsibility to be exercised by the government. They promptly accused the City Inspector's department of corruption and objected to the fact that his duties included "sanitation, regulation of public markets, and inspection of weights and measures, as well as health." They urged to

---

[107] From the 1856 report of the New York State Tenant House Committee, which investigated slum conditions in Brooklyn and New York quoted in Lubove p. 10.
[108] Charles E. Rosenberg. <u>The Cholera Years</u>. Chicago: University of Chicago Press, 1962, p. 121.
[109] Lubove, p. 25.

"establish public health as a specialized function in the complex urban community, a specialization they regarded as a prerequisite to efficient and scientific administration."[110]

These attempts to carve a niche within the medical profession that would deal exclusively with sanitation and its effect on public health were prompted by a new scientific understanding of how contagious diseases were transmitted. British social reformer Edwin Chadwick was first to promote a "sanitary" idea in 1842. His report sought to explain to a wider audience what doctors, health inspectors, and the poor themselves already knew. The poor were sick and died more frequently and at a younger age than the better-off. The obvious difference between their living conditions, he argued, was the filth of their streets and neighborhoods. There must be a causal connection, Chadwick insisted, and filth must be causing sickness and deaths. Therefore, he concluded, if we remove the cause, the effect will go away too.[111]

The American housing reformer utilized ideas from the nascent science of bacteriology. The germ theory "supported his contention that the overcrowding, the primitive waste disposal facilities, and the inadequate lighting and ventilation of tenements took a heavy toll in life and health." In addition to public fear, the success of housing reformers after 1890 was rooted in a better scientific understanding of how diphtheria, pneumonia, and tuberculosis originated and were transmitted in the tenements.[112]

At the same time, the policing of the city was influenced by new ideas in public administration. During the 1860s, many big cities embraced the London model of metropolitan police by adopting military titles and uniforms for their patrolmen. The change was prompted by the new

---

[110] Lubove, p. 15.
[111] Priti Joshi "The Dual Work of 'Wastes' in Chadwick's *Sanitary Report*" at http://humwww.ucsc.edu/dickens/OMF/joshi.html.
[112] Lubove, p. 88.

respect and stature afforded to the military and by the necessity to curb problems worsened by the wartime turmoil. Riots and demonstrations could no longer be handled by regular watchmen.[113] While the novelties were welcomed by the administrators and citizens seeking to make the police force more disciplined and efficient, they were not universally well-received, especially by the patrolman himself. The military uniform made him immediately identifiable to the public and thus hampered his ability to detect crime while keeping his anonymity. (Later, this led to plain-clothes detectives—another sign of specialization.) No less importantly, the uniform made the patrolman an extended arm of the city government present on the streets and thus available for services other than those of maintaining order. It may be surprising to us to learn that many police officers quit their jobs at the time, refusing to wear what they called "servants' livery."[114]

The New York Tenement law is another example of a whole having reached a critical size and breaking into parts. This time, though, the break was along the class lines. The big city broke into smaller areas, in which what was true for one (filth, disease, and trouble) was not necessarily true for another. The Tenement House Law was meant to help abate unhealthy conditions in tenements, but not in single family homes. One was the shelter of the poor; the other, the castle of the middle class. The reformers advocating for the law believed that improving the housing of the poor would eventually reduce class and ethnic conflicts.[115] But inasmuch as they were different classes, the law was an instrument serving one class by coercing another. What was enforcement against the poor was order protection for the rich.

---

[113] Lane, p. 118. As far as the military titles are concerned, they may be seen as signs of meritorious layering. We should recall that today's code enforcement officers are also given different ranks that allow the organization to designate and reward them for their levels of professional knowledge and years of service.

[114] This instance that took place in the Philadelphia police force is cited in Monkkonen, p. 100.

[115] Lubove, p. 42.

At the same time, people living in tenements themselves became, as noted by Roger Lane, "markedly dependent upon authority, inclined to turn to law and government in situations which had earlier been handled informally."[116] Lane also makes another observation quite important for the discussion: when the Boston police department was reorganized and became more efficient, the number of men now available allowed the city to expand their activities. "Some of the new duties," wrote Lane, "were merely odd jobs, as when members of the force were used as messengers to deliver official reports. Others were extensions of existing practices. The men had always helped to provide emergency aid to the unfortunate, for example, [but in] the later 1840s this service was made official."[117]

Here, time and time again, we notice the same principles at work. First, the principle of the expansion by convenience: "We already have all those people on the streets, why don't we have them deliver reports?" Second, a service expanded by convenience soon becomes a specialized duty, and an expected one. Overall, as the lines connecting urban dwellers and their local government deepened through use, there seems to have been a pattern of self-replicating, or self-feeding: the more services were offered, the more services were expected. As it was so succinctly expressed by Roger Lane, "the existence of a strengthened instrument of police created demands for its exercise."[118]

Historian Eric Monkkonen echoes this idea of the increased dependency on city government and the expansion of its services when he writes that "the range of specific activities the police engaged in so multiplied and ramified that it must often have seemed that their least important activity was crime control." But, Monkkonen adds, along with the multiplications of police duties came the taking away of some of their duties by others who would now specialize in them. "Jobs that

---

[116] Lane, p. 2.
[117] Ibid., p. 61.
[118] Lane, p. 39.

the police had originated on a regular basis in the 1850s and 1860s and that devolved to specialists by the turn of the century included a wide range of activities, from health and boiler inspections to the detection and protection of abused children."[119]

Increasingly, then, throughout the nineteenth century the city government found itself in the position of a Boston watchman lighting gas lamps *and* wearing a servant livery. Its role in maintaining order became more complex, broke into specialized areas, and included service functions to both rich and poor. Perhaps it was simply another example of the expansion by convenience, but this time it applied to the government as a whole: "Listen, government, you are already there, why don't you do something else as well?"

---

[119] Both quotations are from Monkkonen, pp. 101-102.

12

HOW WE EXPERIENCE ORDER

If I could express the main idea of this book in a paragraph, I would say that code enforcement emerged as city governments adopted a more proactive and forceful approach to communal order. Order, as we have seen, is not a concept frozen in time. It changes depending on the events threatening it, and it expands more often than it contracts. Code enforcement appeared as a result of such an expansion that intensified in the late-19th century and reached its peak in the 20th.

We experience order in our daily life as a three-level concept. At its first level, order stands for a safe *physical* environment. It means buildings and structures that protect us from the elements and do not collapse. Order means the absence of sharp objects around us that can cut our skin. It means having doors that do not trap us inside and having windows letting in air and light so we diurnal creatures can live and function. Order means smooth surfaces that do not break our ankles as we walk on them. This seems to be a straightforward evolutionary explanation.

Order also means something more subtle than this—and this is its second level—namely, having an environment that is *inoffensive* to our senses. This level of orderliness implies we should see no trash, hear no harsh sounds, smell no toxic fumes. We see here a certain progression towards refinement, as we move from physical safety to the care of our senses not being offended. There is a clear difference between the two. Physically unsafe conditions can harm or kill our bodies. But things offensive to the senses cannot. Why are they offensive, then? Another simple, evolutionary explanation may be that the senses detect harmful things from a distance, before they can reach our body so that contact can be avoided. They are sentries on the watchtowers warning us about dangers. The view of a desolate desert, for example, is unpleasant. Do not go there, our senses tell us, the lack of water means death. The view of a lush oasis, on the other hand, is pleasing. Our senses tell us, Go there, you will find water that will support your life. For the same reason, we find the smell of certain things unpleasant *before* we put them in the mouth; we find the sound of certain things unpleasant *before* we approach them; we find certain surfaces unpleasant to the touch *before* we grab them. If this explanation is correct, the second level of orderliness is there simply to serve the first. We want the environment that would not offend our senses and thus would not be even potentially dangerous to our bodies. This is why we strive for this second level of order.

But now I suggest that there is a third level of order at which we expect our senses not only to be unoffended but to be pleased. We expect beautiful architecture, harmonious art and sculpture, melodious music, fragrant smells, soft surfaces. Here too, we see a form of refinement, for we have moved from the merely inoffensive to the actively pleasing. To provide physical safety only, a building does not need to be decorated; it can be simply a box made of steel and concrete. Yet it is not as conducive to human habitation as a decorated one. Some decorations may be pleasing because they are depictions of pleasing things. If a blank wall of a building is painted as blue skies, peaceful rivers, or green forests, it is pleasing because these things are pleasing by themselves. We like to see them in real life, and their depictions make an otherwise faceless wall more relatable. If this were the only reason for decorating out buildings, the third level of order—the aesthetic pleasing for the eye—would simply be in service of the second and first. But we also adorn blank walls with abstract images too, such as abstract geometric figures—lines, circles, triangles—that do not depict to anything relatable or promising the comfort of the body. It is not clear why. My guess is that what we call aesthetically beautiful, all these decorations including geometric figures, remind us of the universal order, and this is the reason we want them around us.

When we search for order consciously, we easily find its signs everywhere. We see it in the orderly movement of the planets and stars. We hear it in the rhythm of our own hearts. We act it out in the patterns of our daily conduct. But subconsciously, I argue, we too search for order. We search for what lies behind our sensory experience. We search, in other words, for the underlying structure of reality itself, for we suspect, reasonably, that behind the surface veneer which we experience through the senses must exist The Order that maintains and supports it. Behind the paint on the house wall is stucco; behind the stucco is a plywood board; behind the board are studs. Something behind the surface holds it together. As it would be impossible for the paint to hang on thin air, it seems unlikely that behind the perceivable order of things is nothing. It is that universal order that we look for.

When we are able to trace any evidence of what is behind, we try to capture and hold on to it as if it may slip away again. We capture it in the best form available to us. Sometimes it is in images. Sometimes it is in sounds of music. Sometimes it is language. The language of mathematics is one such form, and it is perhaps the most remarkable of them all. Not merely because it appears to be the most precise, but it is remarkable because of our very ability to use it. For the fact that we can express physical laws governing the universe—space, motion, gravity, light—in mathematical formulas suggests that the universal laws are, somehow, meant to be understood by us. It seems that they want to be known to human beings.

Ordinary human speech is the most accessible form in which we express the universal order. It uses words, strings them into sentences, and develops complex and elaborate lines of thinking about reality. In doing so, speech is a mirror reflecting the universal order which it finds outside of itself and independent of itself. But to the degree that reality is orderly, speech as its reflection must be orderly too. And this is, in fact, what we find it to be. Our sentences have structure, our words flow in order, our lines of thinking have internal coherence. The are non-contradictory and operate in terms of cause and effect. Without these features, speech would turn into incomprehensible ramblings. Speech is rational to the degree in which it reflects the universal order.

Finally, we seek to express order through art. "[I]t must never be forgotten," wrote historian Paul Johnson, "that art was instinctively created by humanity to assist the process of ordering, and so understanding and mastering, the wild world of nature. Art is fundamentally about order."[120] My point is that aside from imposing order upon chaotic nature and thus mastering it, men and society as a whole at some point seek to create art to express its commitment to the universal order. This is why we need decoration and adornment, no matter how primitive or practically useless. We need them to remind ourselves of the universal order that we suspect underline reality. We call them beautiful to the degree that they relate to and participate in the universal order.

The three layers of order I described have an obvious hierarchy. What starts with the basic physical needs ends with elevated aesthetic needs. If this reminds the reader of the Maslow pyramid of human needs, the reader is correct. Following Maslow's insight, I too believe in what seems obvious: once human beings secure their basic needs, they begin to beautify their environment. Once they feel safe and well fed, they use their limited energy to expand rapidly from the first level to the second and the third. Once society has enough resources, it does the same. Order expands as people seek its highest universal form.

Is local government in the position to help with that? Whether it is or isn't, in the 20th century it tried.

---

[120] Paul Johnson, <u>Art: A New History</u>. HarperCollins Publishers Inc., 2003, p. 5.

13
THE BIRTH OF CITY PLANNING

*As the actual physical power of government increased,
many citizens caught glimpses of an even greater potential.
In combining older ideas of the authority of the state with
a nineteenth-century faith in progress, they enlarged their
expectations and hoped to use the law not merely to control
behavior but forcibly to improve it.*

Roger Lane

Code enforcement appeared as a result of a government expansion on federal, state, and local levels that took place in the 20th century. To understand what happened, we need to look at the end of the 19th.

During the fifty years after the Civil War, the United States turned into the industrial powerhouse it has remained to this day. Not only did old industries remain active and grow larger, there also emerged new forms of production—manufacture of steel and iron, extraction of oil, refinement of petroleum, building of heavy machinery, and generation of electrical power. Industrial growth transformed society. Internal and external migration increased urban population; new modes of transportation, from horses to boats to railway trains, connected formerly remote places and engaged them in the larger economy; mastery of electricity and new piping materials made it possible to build elevators and deliver water under pressure to higher floors, leading to the construction of high-rises; new partnerships between government and big business allowed acquisition to transfer of large tracks of land through eminent domain. A new class of industrialists emerged, followed by a prosperous middle class and a blue-collar working class.

Another transformation was the use of mass media. 19th-century reformers needed allies to help them change the way cities responded to the tenement problems. The physicians, who had professional expertise and eyewitness knowledge of the conditions, were a great resource. But in addition, the reformers acquired a special ally to mobilize public opinion: the press. From the second half of the nineteenth century on, journalists and writers (from Harriet Beecher Stowe to Horace Greely, Lincoln Steffens, and later Rachel Carson) would play an increasingly prominent role influencing the public opinion and by extension democratic politics. The nature of local news reporting then, as it is now, was to concentrate on the most thrilling events happening as close as possible to the reader. The first cheap "penny" paper published daily was founded in 1831 in Boston; soon, however, a number of them appeared in every big city, competing with the older and more established publications. The "penny" papers found it more advantageous to leave state and national matters to their bigger rivals. Instead, they focused on the local news which the others ignored. Especially helpful for the sale of the dailies were the reports of violent and exciting incidents. The more violent, the louder paperboys could shout. Such reports, wrote Roger Lane, could be gathered most easily each morning in the court. This genre of police court reportage became so popular that soon even the more conservative press had to adopt it.[121] This cheap but effective way of disseminating shocking information turned some of the reporters into star players in the late 19th century's fight against slums. If the goal was to find shock and scandal, the city slums were the place to look.

Just as in the 1960s Rachel Carson's *Silent Spring* was credited with the spurring of the environmental protection laws, the "muckrakers," as they were called, energized public opinion in the late 19th century. The reading tastes had already begun adapting to the more naturalistic style of writing. The descriptive literature on industrial and working-class conditions, such as Lincoln Steffens's *Shame of the Cities*, Ida Tarbell's *History of the Standard Oil Company*, and Upton Sinclair's *The Jungle* sent shock waves through the now-more-educated and affluent society. For the housing reformers seeking

---

[121] Lane, p. 48.

ways to push the city government to accept its responsibility over slum conditions, Jacob Riis's book *How the Other Half Lives* published in 1890 was destined to become an indispensable tool. Featuring powerful photographs showing the dwellers of alleys and tenements, the book is still in print today.

The reformers of the late 19th and early 20th centuries called themselves Progressives. The movement they formed aimed at improving the living and working conditions of the poor, but also at cleaning up inefficient city governments. The Federal Civil Service Reform of 1883 ended the practice of giving away federal jobs for political patronage and placed federal employees on the merit system. It also resulted in the founding of the National Municipal League in 1894 that included reformers from different parts of the country and led to the downfall of the corrupt political machines of Chicago, Baltimore, and New York. In the same year, the first National Conference for Good City Government was held where academics and reformers looked for ways to strengthen municipal operations. A prominent writer of the time, Herbert Croly, wrote that the Progressive movement symbolized "the decision of a considerable number of citizens that we could no longer rely simply upon great natural wealth and complete individual freedom to fulfill the American dream of economic independence."[122] The role of government was understood as having to be bigger, more assertive, and more constructive than ever before.

The field of public administration began professionalizing. To use Dwight Waldo's expression, it became self-aware. (We should remember this concept, because in many ways today's code enforcement has become self-aware too.) Waldo's understanding of the Progressive movement is worth reproducing in full:

> The economic and political formulae of classical economics became, perhaps, a useful Myth for the period in which they were elaborated; many people found them helpful, and they

---

[122] *The Promise of American Life*, quoted in Dwight Waldo, *The Administrative State*. The Ronald Press Company, 1948, p. 5.

produced some manifest blessings. But the postulate that there is a harmony of nature, which if undisturbed would be productive of the greatest good of the greatest number, lost its appeal for many thoughtful and sensitive people with the passing of time and the altering of circumstances. The increasing ratio of population to resources, the vastness of waste and confusion, the failure of the traditional ways to produce a tolerable life for large numbers of our population even in the midst of plenty—these led an ever-increasing number of academic, literary, and civic-minded people to abandon the old faith in a natural harmony in favor of a new ideal: that of a man-made harmony.[123]

The vision of a man-made harmony was a manifestation of what was discussed earlier: the confidence of the scientific mind in man's ability to change the world. The belief in progress and science was trendy; it was *avant-garde* to see the future as being meticulously engineered and skillfully wrought—like a well-built machine. In the context of public administration, harmony was to be created through a strong instrumentality of government bureaucracy. The human community of the future would be reinvented: it would be carefully planned and scientifically administered. Combined with advanced building technology and now professionalized architects, engineers, and transportation specialists, the idea brought to life a new occupation—the city planner.

Constance McLaughlin Green explained that city planning received its early momentum in Chicago when a group of architects, sculptors, and landscapers were commissioned to lay out the fairgrounds for the Columbian Exposition of 1893. When the Exposition opened, local promoters and visitors alike were awed and overwhelmed by the beauty of what they saw: the "White City" built south of Chicago. The opening of the Exposition can be said to be the

---

[123] Ibid, pp. 4-5.

moment when a new movement called the City Beautiful was born. If a handful of creative professionals could build within the short time of a year such a place, the thinking was, others could do the same. Soon, cities from coast to coast started preparing plans to purchase land and make improvements that would improve their appearances.[124]

The City Beautiful movement originated ideas and crystallized approaches that prevailed throughout the twentieth century. First, cities took a proactive stance towards urban problems. Rather than wait for the next crisis and try to solve problems after they become intolerable, why not prevent them? Second, why not create urban order on a large scale the way we want it to be? The rational, scientific approach should be able to do that. Third, for the first time on such a scale, the government became a partner in the development of large tracts of land. After an 1896 Supreme Court decision in *Chicago, Burlington & Quincy Railroad Co. v. City of Chicago* throughout the twentieth century projects that began as private ventures often ended up turning to government powers of eminent domain to complete them. This was the only way by which they could acquire private land from unwilling sellers. Fourth, for the first time American society was affluent enough to afford not merely buying land and developing it but to make it a priority to create beauty *on a large, public scale*. In short, at the end of the nineteenth century it seemed that the "city upon a hill" was possible once again; this time not through the devotion to God but through the reason of Man.

Lawrence Kennedy described how in the early twentieth century, city planning consolidated into a new field, and how engineers and architects stepped forward to assert the ideals and accept the title of a professional planner. The first national conference on planning was held in Washington, D.C. in 1909. In the same year the first course in planning was offered at Harvard and the first textbook in the field printed.[125] It is also important to note how the aims of the new

---

[124] Green, p. 126.

[125] Lawrence W. Kennedy. <u>Planning the City upon a Hill: Boston since 1630</u>. Amherst: University of Massachusetts Press, 1992, p. 124.

profession were formulated. In 1910, at the second planning conference, Frederick Law Olmsted, Jr., a leading figure in the movement, used the word *harmony* to assert that

> all the planning that shapes each of the fragments that go to make up the physical city shall be so harmonized as to reduce the conflict of purposes and the waste of constructive effort to a minimum, and thus secure for the people of the city conditions adapted to their attaining the maximum of productive efficiency, of health, and of enjoyment of life.[126]

The attentive reader will notice that in this well-articulated vision, there is no mention of public safety—nothing about riots, fire, or epidemics. By the early 20th century, those ills were already being handled by other professionals. Instead, the city planner was to focus on maximizing productive efficiency (implying that some efficiency must have been there already), health and, importantly, the enjoyment of life.

Any form of professionalism has a built-in self-prophecy. To be a professional in the 20th century meant a lifetime of learning. But, in a self-propelling dynamic, once a person dedicates his life to a field of knowledge, he necessarily enriches the field. The field of knowledge benefits and deepens by being a center of attention of so many dedicated professionals. When city planners came to the fore, it was only a matter of time before they would begin developing their own professional standards of good and bad, of beautiful and ugly. The idea of the "enjoyment of life" (however open to interpretation it may be) has found its embodiment in a new chapter of municipal law we now call zoning regulations. From the planner's standpoint it meant that the buildings, streets and grounds of the city ought not only to be functional but also beautiful. This means that *in addition* to measurable development standards (for example, the height and

---

[126] Quoted in Kennedy, p. 124.

location of a structure on the site), zoning regulations must at some point inevitably include aesthetic values.

The modern developer expects as a matter of course that when he brings his plans for city approval, they will be reviewed by an urban designer. This was not always the case. In the past, if beautiful structures were built, it was mostly through private effort and without government involvement.[127] It is only in the twentieth century that a full-time city employee reviews architectural design and has the power to approve or reject it. For the first time, then, with the appearance of the city planner as a dedicated professional, American municipalities became involved, in addition to the matters of basic safety, in the matters of aesthetics. Other professionals will deal with protecting life from epidemics and fire; as far as the planner is concerned, once life is not threatened, it may as well have *quality* to it. It may as well be beautiful. The affluence of society allows the planner to interpret quality of life very broadly and to consider beauty as a prerequisite. As suggested earlier in the Philadelphia fountains phenomenon, the definition of urban order has expanded once again, now to include beauty.

In their 1963 book *Man-Made America: Chaos or Control?* two professional planners, Christopher Tunnard and Boris Pushkarev, summarized how, by that time, aesthetic standards made their way into communal thinking and consequently into law. They wrote that for a long time prior any questions of aesthetics were of private concern. They quote a judge who wrote, in 1905, that aesthetic considerations were a matter of "luxury and indulgence rather than of necessity."

---

[127] This is how Lawrence Kennedy expressed this idea: "In the early years of the seventeenth century, the physical community and built environment simply evolved from the aggregate of decisions made by individuals. Private citizens designed homes and workplaces; private partnerships provided basic services; and the extent of government involvement in city planning was limited to the Great and General Court of the Commonwealth [of Massachusetts], which enacted the necessary legislation. Private entrepreneurs orchestrated major developments, such as filling in the shoreline and building the early wharves." Kennedy, p. 4.

When trees were planted on a street, it was done by private philanthropy, not through public action. Every man's house was his castle, and the judge knew of no case law that held that someone may be deprived of their property because his tastes are not those of his neighbor. "Since then," wrote the planners, "the interpretation of public welfare and interest has changed, and aesthetic considerations have managed to get a legal foothold." The beauty of surroundings is an appropriate consideration within the statutory criterion of the general welfare. "Through planning," they conclude, "it should be possible to make our physical surroundings attractive, so that community beauty is the rule rather than the exception.[128]

There is undeniable logic behind all this. As should be obvious by now, the planner may justifiably insist that (using the principle of expansion by convenience) if one spends time and resources designing a building, one might as well spend a little more and make it beautiful so that the whole neighborhood would benefit from it. Thus, true to his calling, the city planner has stood guard to promote urban beauty since the early 20th century. It should be obvious by now who would become his sword and shield. As has been repeated in this book, code enforcement is a broad field where its multiple duties often overlap with those of others'—the fire inspector, the health inspector, the police officer. But the trick is to look where the duties do *not* overlap. The trick is to ask, What is it that code enforcement does that is unique? The answer is that, uniquely among others, it enforces zoning regulations. Code enforcement would not be here today if it were not for this relatively new focus on order and beauty on a large, city-wide scale.

---

[128] Christopher Tunnard and Boris Pushkarev. <u>Man-Made America: Chaos or Control?</u> New Haven and London: Yale University Press, 1963, p. 405-406.

14
20TH-CENTURY KNOWLEDGE AND CREATIVITY

Although not in the name, but in the spirit the City Beautiful movement lives on in the 21st century. Social reformers of the past kept looking for a causal connection between the physical environment and urban ills. This has not changed. Similar to the 19th-century housing reformer, who assumed that by improving housing conditions they would influence the character of the slum dweller, the planner's ideal— a well-designed and beautiful city—promises a more productive, healthier population, ready for the enjoyment of life.

No one could argue that the planner is mistaken. If the early reformer could look at our cities today, he would indeed see them as much more enjoyable. Thanks to the strengthened municipal laws, including building and zoning regulations that have controlled construction and development for at least a hundred-eighty years, the physical environment we live in, even in the most disadvantaged neighborhoods, is much less dangerous, if at all, to human life and health. It is true that even today there are run-down neighborhoods with structures so dilapidated as to be dangerous to their occupants. In the early 2000s, a Los Angeles apartment building collapsed leaving dozens of families stranded. The cause of the collapse was thought to be termite damage not detected and fixed on time.[129] In 2021 a 12-story condominium building in Miami partially collapsed, killing 98 people. The high-rise was built in 1981. But incidents like this are rare, and if people die early deaths in our run-down areas, it is more often from a

---

[129] *The Los Angeles Times,* December 26, 2000.

stray bullet than a collapsed building. The physical environment itself has become immeasurably more conducive to human flourishing: there are no more open ditches or cesspools, dwellings are built with provisions for light and ventilation, there is plenty of clean water, both hot and cold, residential streets and alleys are paved, trash and garbage are collected on a regular basis, and few people remember what privy vaults were.

But has the urban dweller started enjoying life more? It does not seem so. The more care is given to urban order and the more its definition expands, the more vulnerable the order seems to be in the eyes of many. Not that the old threats to it are so persistent, but rather there are new threats are being identified all the time, popping up here and there, forcing the definition of communal order to expand even more to include fresh prohibitions. If judged by news reports, life today is filled with crises, just as it was reported in the 19th-century penny papers. That might surprise and even disappoint the early reformer. Could it be, he might muse, that a macro definition of urban order, that is, one that keeps expanding and expanding, leads to a micro definition of crisis...?

As before, the increased number of concerns that communities have today do translate into more regulatory services provided by their cities. It is not a paradox that the more affluent a society becomes, the more enforcement personnel are demanded. As has been shown, at first society learns how to eliminate basic dangers: fires, epidemics, and riots; and once this is done, it moves on aiming at other, loftier and subtler, goals. While the fire inspector, the health inspector, and the police officer have not gone away; while they still shield us from basic dangers, the attainment of new goals is done through others. This is how anti-smoking, lead-based paint, environmental protection, occupational safety, excessive noise, noxious smells, and dozens of other regulations have brought to life specialized inspectors.

This is how, among many other of its duties, code enforcement does its work to preserve historic buildings regulations or other non-safety laws initiated by planning departments. The 1975 Act Establishing the Boston Landmarks Commission proclaimed that one of its purposes was "to protect the beauty of the city of Boston and improve the quality of its environment through [. . .] maintenance" of its historic sites. Whoever violated the Act was to be punished (in 1975) by a fine of not less than fifty dollars nor more than five hundred dollars. It was a specialized unit of the housing inspectors that began enforcing this law.

As has been discussed already, the need to beautify one's environment is ever present in human endeavors, although it may not be the first thing one has in mind thinking about one's needs. If Abraham Maslow's theory works on an individual level, it seems to work on a societal level as well. "At once other (and higher) needs emerge," wrote Maslow, "and these, rather than physiological hungers, dominate the organism. And when these in turn are satisfied, again new (and still higher) needs emerge, and so on. As one desire is satisfied, another pops up to take its place."[130] It may be that once the basic threats to order are perceived to be under control, society as an aggregate of individual needs begins pursuing other needs, those of a higher order. And on this higher level of order the beautiful occupies its rightful place.

If this is true, we come to the uneasy supposition that perhaps human needs may never be satisfied. Once again, it seems, the city upon a hill turns out to be unachievable. To borrow a concept from the world of physics again, the closer a particle in the accelerator gets to the speed of light, the more difficult and eventually impossible it is for the particle to achieve the speed. Writing about city riots in the late 1960s, political scientist Edward Banfield offered a profound insight that illustrates the same point only as it applies to society. For an upwardly mobile and politically minded person, he wrote, "who has a potential for outbursts of righteous indignation and for demonstrations, even serious and successful efforts at reform are likely to leave him more rather than less angry.

---

[130] Abraham Maslow "A theory of human motivation." Psychological Review, 50 (4), 1943, 375.

The faster and farther [he] rises the more impatient he is likely to be with whatever he thinks prevents his rising still faster and still farther. [...] The process of "middle-" and "upper-classification" [of the poor] is making the whole society more sensitive to departures, both real and imaginary, from the ideal, inherently unrealizable, of how things ought to be. As the economy becomes more productive and social arrangements more decent, the well-off—and among them youth especially—become more restless and more intolerant of the continual failure to achieve social perfection. Demonstrations, confrontations, protests, dialogues, and so forth, are bound to be more frequent as the middle and upper classes grow and more and more people have the leisure to act upon what the Judaeo-Puritan tradition tells them is a positive obligation to make society over.[131]

Indeed, modern demands of and expectations from urban life have grown larger. The notion of urban blight as it was understood by the early reformer has not gone away—a dilapidated building is still an eye sore, and a pile of trash is still a pile of trash—but it has grown to include more items. There appears to be, on the part of today's urban dwellers, a new and heightened sensitivity to their environment: they are more attentive to and less tolerant of smaller irritants. Their perception of what orderly life should be has become more sophisticated. Aside from the philosophic reasons explaining man as ever-aspiring to the universal order, there may also be more earthly economic reasons for such a refinement of tastes.

Since the late 19th century, the level of education and professionalization has grown so much that America became, in the expression of organizational management luminary Peter Drucker, a "knowledge society." The methods of production changed: machines

---

[131] Edward C. Banfield. "Rioting Mainly for Fun and Profit" in The Metropolitan Enigma. James Q. Wilson, Ed. Anchor Books, 1970, pp. 336-337.

have replaced practically all aspects of manual labor, knowledge turned into the driving force of the economy, and "human capital" became most valuable. Economist Thomas Sowell wrote that in the 20th century those who could contribute only physical labor had difficulties finding jobs in a high-technology world. In this new world, skills were rewarded mostly highly, not strong backs.[132]

Sowell also pointed out another contributing factor worthy of our attention. "This economic de-emphasis of physical strength," he wrote, "also had the side-effect of reducing or eliminating the advantage of male workers over female workers."[133] It is not a far step to suppose that the more prominent role the women have played in the American economy, its social and political life, the more their natural sophistication has contributed to the refinement of our common tastes. It would be surprising if the heightened sensitivity of the 50% of the population, now much more outspoken than ever before, were not a driver towards an expanded communal order.[134]

Another factor driving the heightened sensitivity, in the observation of Richard Florida, is the rise of a creative class. Its roots can be traced, wrote Florida, to the mid-20th century during which time new economic systems were explicitly designed "to foster and harness human creativity, and the emergence of a new social milieu that supports it. And it has given rise to a new dominant class."[135] Florida argued that it was no longer knowledge, as Drucker had thought, but its superior sister, *creativity*, that was now driving the American economy. Consider the numbers Florida gives in his book:

> The growth of the scientific and technically creative workforce becomes even clearer when we account for the growth in

---

[132] Thomas Sowell. <u>Basic Economics: A Citizen's Guide to the Economy</u>. NY: Basic Books, 2000, p. 342.

[133] Ibid.

[134] On women's sensitivity see, for example, Fischer, Agneta H et al. "Gender differences in emotion perception and self-reported emotional intelligence: A test of the emotion sensitivity hypothesis." *PloS one* vol. 13,1 e0190712. 25 Jan. 2018.

[135] Richard Florida. <u>The Rise of the Creative Class</u>. NY: Basic Books, 2002, p. 66.

population. In 1900, there were just 55 scientists and engineers for every 100,000 people in the United States. That figure increased to 400 by 1950, and to more than 1,000 in 1980. By 1999 there were more than 1,800 scientists and engineers per 100,000 people. The numbers of people making a living from artistic and cultural creativity also expanded dramatically over the course of the past century, and particularly since 1950. Professional artists, writers and performers—so-called "bohemians"—increased from some 200,000 in 1900 to 525,000 in 1950 and to 2.5 million in 1999, an increase of more than 375 percent since 1950. There were roughly 250 bohemians for every 100,000 Americans in 1900, a figure that increased to roughly 350 by 1950. That number crossed 500 in 1980, before reaching 900 for every 100,000 Americans in 1999.[136]

Given the numbers, it is small wonder that the 21st century urbanites display a finer sense of order in their environment and demand a more persnickety form of enforcement.

The typical municipality has had no choice but to respond, and rather quickly, for one of the characteristics of the modern workforce is its high mobility. To maintain their tax base and stimulate economic development, cities have had to compete among each other for the knowledge and creative workers and for the companies who hire them. Urban policy experts Edward Blakely and Ted Bradshaw emphasized that the quality of the environment has a great effect on where a modern worker decides to live. Especially, people involved in research and development—that is, knowledge and creative workers—choose to live in residential environments with high-quality amenities, cultural venues, commercial hubs, social gatherings, and educational facilities. It applies even more to executives and managerial personnel. High salaries are important, but are not as likely to entice people to a location where

---

[136] Ibid., pp. 45-46.

the quality of the environment appears poor. The most obvious way in which to stimulate economic development of a city is to create a quality environment where people will live in "an orderly, well-maintained community proud of itself.[137]

The typical municipality has not taken any chances. Driven by professionals from different fields of knowledge it now takes a much more *proactive* stance in identifying dangers to order. It denotes urban blight not only as dilapidated buildings: in today's language urban blight also means abandoned vehicles, dumped furniture, graffiti, and broken windows. And even though these conditions, unlike a decrepit home, cannot harm anyone directly, society has learned to recognize in them the early signs of decay. We now know that broken windows may lead to more serious troubles for the neighborhood, even increased crime and drug-related activities. More sensitive to these early symptoms, we want to cure them before the disease takes over. "Just as physicians now recognize the importance of fostering health rather than simply treating illness, so the police—and the rest of us—ought to recognize the importance of maintaining, intact, communities without broken windows."[138]

And what about beauty? How can the municipality ensure that properties are not just maintained to the minimum, but new, attractive buildings and public projects are built? The creation of beautiful objects requires disposable resources. The creation of monumental beauty on an urban scale requires *large* disposable resources. A democratic form of government is not necessarily best-suited for such a purpose. In it, power and resources are dispersed among many players rather than being concentrated in the hands of a few. Historian John

---

[137] Edward J. Blakely and Ted K. Bradshaw. <u>Planning Local Economic Development: Theory and Practice.</u> Thousand Oaks, CA: Sage Publications, 2002, pp. 213 and 365-366.

[138] James Q. Wilson and George L. Kelling. "Broken Windows." *Atlantic Monthly*, March 1982. For an alternative view, see Bernard E. Harcourt. <u>Illusion of Order: The False Promise of Broken Windows Policing</u>. Cambridge, MA: Harvard University Press, 2001.

Burchard noted that "moments of great urban beauty have often, indeed usually, been achieved by dictatorial decisions." Places such as St. Peter's Square in Rome or the Place de la Concorde in Paris emerged when "an autocrat with taste found an architect of genius." The democratic substitute for this is not easy to find.[139] This is especially true for the American kind of democracy where municipal decisions (both on the elective and administrative level) entail negotiation, bargaining, and compromise. Then, can our cities be beautiful? They can and sometimes are. And the increased number of laws and regulators, especially in the area of planning, are nothing else but well-intentioned and highly professional attempts to make our environment not only physically safe but also visually attractive.

As always, however, there is a price to pay. In the American city, the price is individual freedom. Hardly noticeable to those who live through the change (let this be repeated once again), but better noticeable to an outsider, American freedom is giving way to more regulation in the name of an ideal communal order. Like the magic chagrin skin in Balzac's novel, which slowly disappeared in front of the main character's eyes with every wish granted to him, perhaps you can have either one, but not both. Order always detracts from freedom, just as freedom always undermines order. The ever-delicate balance between the two, at least at this point, appears to be tipping towards order. Could this be a promise of a beautiful future?

---

[139] John Burchard. "Design and Urban Beauty in the Central City" in <u>The Metropolitan Enigma.</u> James Q. Wilson, ed. Anchor Books, 1970, p. 231.

15
WHERE IS SOCIETY'S HEART?

*A theory is a good theory if it satisfies two requirements.
It must accurately describe a large class of observations
on the basis of a model that contains only few arbitrary
elements, and it must make definite predictions
about the results of future observations.*

Stephen Hawking

In the beginning I posed a simple but slightly arrogant question: Why do we have code enforcement in today's municipality? I say it was an arrogant question because the assumption was that an answer to the question existed and could be found. But now, at the end, for all we know, the question may simply be unanswerable. Just like the question "What is the building block of the universe?" has been, and may always be, unanswerable. The closer we peer into the more and more powerful microscope, the more complex, not simpler, the tiniest elements of life appear to us. We look for answers but only find more questions. Perhaps one must accept that if the previous pages have not been able to present a clear and distinct picture of how code enforcement came to be, they have at least offered a pastel sketch of the developments leading to it.

We have discovered that we can identify with more or less precision when and where the *functions* that are now performed by code enforcement originated, but not code enforcement itself. Those places and times turned out to be, prosaically, where and when small settlements began growing. This is hardly a revolutionary discovery. This simply means that *wherever* and *whenever* human settlements begin to grow, some form of order maintenance begins to emerge. It would be almost impossible, then, to identify when or where exactly code enforcement as we know it today started, just as it would be impossible to determine where the great Mississippi River starts. Like any complex phenomenon in life, it is a confluence of many other phenomena.

Still, at least one firm marker can be offered. Year 1983 may very well be designated as its birth year because it was then that an entire issue of a scholarly journal was dedicated exclusively to code enforcement.[140] The issue included ten articles providing a general overview of code enforcement; descriptions of housing programs in eleven cities; analysis of code enforcement in San Francisco, Los Angeles, Indianapolis, and Kirkland; a report on the operation of a dedicated housing court; description of challenges of applying new fire safety laws to existing buildings; and an argument in favor of code enforcement to minimize municipal liability. One of its authors usefully defined a code enforcement system as having specific elements: a housing code; a regulatory agency charged with doing housing inspections and enforcing the code; a special housing court adjudicating code enforcement cases; a prosecutor for handling cases; and assistance programs to be made available to property owners to bring their buildings into compliance.[141]

This scholarly approach tells us, of course, that by 1983 code enforcement had already existed in many cities; or else there would have been no issue of a journal dedicated to it. We know from municipal records that in New York City, for example, it was 1978 when the housing inspectors began calling their assignments code enforcement. But other than trying to catch words and pin them to the time of their

---

[140] University of Detroit Journal of Urban Law 60, no. 3 (Spring 1983).

[141] Elizabeth Howe, "Housing Code Enforcement in Eleven Cities," University of Detroit Journal of Urban Law 60, no. 3 (Spring 1983), p. 373.

appearance (a futile task), the precise time and place of code enforcement's emergence must remain hidden.

By now the main conclusions of this essay should be obvious. Code enforcement is not a new development in the American municipality. Rather, it is a result of continuous attempts by communities, large and small, to maintain order through the passage and enforcement of its laws. When we look at a specific moment in time—say, sixty years ago—when approximately code enforcement emerged, we find that that in fact it only *crystallized* sixty years ago: it became "self-aware" and assumed a name of its own to distinguish itself from others. However, the duties that code enforcement undertook originated as far back as in Colonial times. In addition, what we call the crystallization of code enforcement into an entity may have been only a temporary re-distribution of enforcement duties between the police, housing inspectors, and other arms of municipal enforcement. As has been shown, code enforcement itself is hardly a frozen entity. It continues to subdivide and re-arrange itself, mixing and merging with other elements of its environment, and popping up again here and there under different names.

The presence of code enforcement as a regulatory arm of local government creates new demands of its exercise as members of the community ask for more services. Code enforcement officers themselves, in their eagerness to be called true professionals, often push to undertake new and important duties. It is not inconceivable, then, that at some point in time code enforcement, or some other branching off or specializing unit, may concentrate on enforcing violations of a purely aesthetic nature.

As far as code enforcement's aspiration for professionalism is concerned, it seems to me that it is unlikely to be realized.[142] Code enforcement may have to remain an occupation without ever becoming a true profession. The reason for my hesitation is the language of the maintenance codes we enforce daily. Just like the phrase "public peace and order" can never be defined precisely, which leaves the patrolman much discretion in interpretation, the code enforcement officer works with a language that is very vague. It bears repeating that the phrases like "accumulation of trash," "dilapidated fence," or "deteriorated structure" are nowhere defined in our municipal codes, because they express communal ideals rather than measurable standards. The maintenance code does not and apparently cannot specify firm standards of compliance. And since the "accumulation of trash," "dilapidated fence," or "deteriorated structure" are open for interpretation, they can and will be a subject of negotiation between the officer, property owner, complaining neighbor, the officer's supervisor, the supervisor's supervisor, and the elected official. Whatever the officer decides can always be overruled by a superior.

The ambiguity of code enforcement work makes it impossible to create a theory of code enforcement, to compress the best practices of code enforcement, or to pass the experience of code enforcement onto others. The knowledge and intuition that make a good officer cannot be transferred from one to another in a structured way in academia. They can only be acquired through experience. Hence the limited prospects of it becoming a profession. It may need to remain a craft.

It has been said that "[h]ow we define the role of police is [...] a direct

---

[142] The following line of thinking draws on the ideas of James Q. Wilson (<u>Bureaucracy: What Government Agencies Do and Why They Do It</u> and <u>Varieties of Police Behavior: The Management of Law and Order in Eight Communities</u>) and of Deborah Stone (<u>Policy Paradox: the art of political decision making</u>).

reflection of society's heart."[143] Expanding this idea into the question of code enforcement and its role in modern America, we may say that, as of today, society's heart appears to be in a peculiar place where it senses the world's imperfections more acutely than ever before. Some may call this sensitivity trifling; some may call it a sign of progress. For better or for worse, if society's heart feels it needs to have more control over its environment, code enforcement's job as public servants is to answer this call.

---

[143] Bryan Vila and Cynthia Morris, eds. <u>The Role of Police in American Society: a documentary history</u>. Westport, CT: Greenwood Press, 1999, p. xxiii.

BIBLIOGRAPHY

Aldridge, Henry R. The National Housing Manual. A Guide to National Housing Policy and Administration. National Housing and Town Planning Council, London, 1923.

Anthrop, Donald F. Noise Pollution. Lexington, Mass.: Lexington Books, 1973.

Banfield, Edward C. "Rioting Mainly for Fun and Profit" in The Metropolitan Enigma. James Q. Wilson, ed. Anchor Books, 1970.

Banfield, Edward C., and James Q. Wilson. City Politics. Cambridge, Mass.: Harvard University Press, 1963.

Blakely, Edward J., Ted K. Bradshaw. Planning Local Economic Development: Theory and Practice. 3rd ed. Thousand Oaks, CA: Sage Publications, 2002.

Bragdon, Clifford R. Noise Pollution: The Unquiet Crisis. Philadelphia: University of Pennsylvania Press, 1970.

Brearley, Harry Chase. <u>Fifty Years of a Civilizing Force</u>. A historical and critical study of the work of the Nationals Board of Fire Underwriters. NY: Frederick A. Stokes company, 1916.

Brogan, Hugh. <u>Longman History of the United States of America</u>. NY: William Morrow and Company, Inc., 1985.

Costello, Augustine E. <u>Our police protectors: history of the New York police from the earliest period to the present time</u>. NY: C.F. Roper, 1885.

Coy, Owen Cochran. <u>Gold Days</u>. Los Angeles, Ca: Powell Publishing Company, 1929.

Earle, Alice Morse. <u>Colonial Days in Old New York</u>. NY: Empire State Book Co., 1926.

Eldredge, Zoeth Skinner. <u>The Beginnings of San Francisco</u>. NY: John C. Rankin Company, 1912.

Elson, Henry William. <u>History of the United States of America</u>, NY: The MacMillan Company, 1904.

Finney, Shan. <u>Noise Pollution: A Scientific and Psychological Look at a New Hazard</u>. NY: Franklin Watts, 1984.

Florida, Richard. <u>The Rise of the Creative Class</u>. NY: Basic Books, 2002.

Ford, James. <u>Slums and Housing: History, Conditions, Policy</u>. Cambridge, Mass.: Harvard University Press, 1936.

Friedman, Lawrence M. <u>Government and Slum Housing: a century of frustration</u>. Chicago: Rand McNally, 1968.

Green, Constance McLaughlin. <u>The Rise of Urban America</u>. NY: Harper & Row Publishers, 1965.

Handlin, Oscar. "The Modern City as a Field of Historical Study" in <u>The Historian and the City</u>, Oscar Handlin and John Burchard, eds. Cambridge, Mass.: The M.I.T. Press, 1963.

Howe, Elizabeth. "Housing Code Enforcement in Eleven Cities." University of Detroit Journal of Urban Law 60, no. 3 (Spring 1983).

____________. "Code Enforcement in Three Cities: An Organizational Analysis." 13 The Urb. Law. 65 (1981).

Hunter, David. <u>The Slums: Challenge and Response</u>. N.Y.: Free Press, 1964.

Joshi, Priti. "The Dual Work of 'Wastes' in Chadwick's *Sanitary Report*" at http://humwww.ucsc.edu/dickens/OMF/joshi.html, accessed on 6-9-3.

Kennedy, Lawrence W. <u>Planning the City upon a Hill: Boston since 1630</u>. Amherst: University of Massachusetts Press, 1992.

Lane, Roger. <u>Policing the City: Boston, 1822-1885.</u> Cambridge, Mass.: Harvard University Press, 1967.

Lubove, Roy. <u>The Progressives And The Slums: Tenement House Reform in New York City, 1890-1917.</u> University of Pittsburgh Press, 1962.

Melosi, Martin V. <u>The Sanitary City: urban infrastructure in America from colonial times to the present.</u> Baltimore, Maryland: The Johns Hopkins University Press, 2000.

Meyerson, Martin, Barbara Terrett, William L.C. Wheaton. <u>Housing, People, and Cities.</u> NY: McGraw-Hill Book Co., 1962.

Monkkonen, Eric H. <u>America Becomes Urban: the development of U.S. cities and towns, 1780-1980.</u> Berkeley and Los Angeles, Ca.: University of California Press, 1988.

<u>National Housing Association (Proceedings of the first National Housing Conference Held in New York, June 3, 5, and 6, 1911).</u> Proceedings of the Academy of Political Science in the City of New York. The Academy of Political Science, Columbia University, New York, 1912.

Navin, Robert B. <u>Analysis of a Slum Area.</u> Washington, D.C.: Catholic University of America, 1934.

Nivola, Pietro S. <u>The Urban Service Problem: a study of housing inspection.</u> Lexington, Mass: Lexington Books, 1979.

Riis, Jacob A. <u>How the Other Half Lives: Studies Among the Tenements of New York</u>. N.Y.: Dover Publications, Inc., 1971.

Robertson, John. <u>Housing and Public Health.</u> NY: Funk & Wagnalls Co., 1920.

Robinson, James Harvey. <u>Medieval and Modern Times.</u> Boston: Ginn & Company, 1916.

Rosenberg, Charles E. <u>The Cholera Years</u>. Chicago: University of Chicago Press, 1962.

__________________. Explaining Epidemics and Other Studies in the History of Medicine. Cambridge University Press, 1992.

Rubinstein, Jonathan. City Police. NY: Farrar, Straus, and Giroux, 1973.

Schilling, Joseph M., James B. Hare. Code Enforcement: A Comprehensive Approach. Solano Press, Point Arena CA, 1995.

Schlesinger, Arthur M. "A Panoramic View: The City in American History" in The City in American Life from Colonial Times to the Present. Paul Kramer and Frederick L. Holborn, eds. NY: G.P. Putnam's Sons, 1970.

Still, Bayrd. "Patterns of Mid-Nineteenth-Century Urbanization in the Middle West" in The City in American Life from Colonial Times to the Present. Paul Kramer and Frederick L. Holborn, eds. NY: G.P. Putnam's Sons, 1970.

Stone, Deborah. Policy Paradox: the art of political decision making. NY: W.W. Norton & Co, 2002.

Taylor, Alan. American Colonies. NY: Viking Penguin, 2001.

Townroe, B.S. The Slum Problem. NY: Longmans, Green & Co., 1928.

Veiller, Lawrence. A Model Housing Law. Russell Sage Foundation, New York, 1920.

Veiller, Lawrence. Housing Reform. NY: Russell Sage, 1910.

Vila, Bryan and Cynthia Morris, eds. The Role of Police in American

Society: a documentary history. Westport, CT: Greenwood Press, 1999.

Waldo, Dwight. The Administrative State. N.Y.: The Ronald Press Company, 1948.

Waldo, Dwight. The Enterprise of Public Administration: A Summary View. Novato, Ca: Chandler & Sharp Publishers, Inc., 1980.

Wilson, James Q. Bureaucracy: What Government Agencies Do and Why They Do It. NY: Basic Books, 1989.

__________. Varieties of Police Behavior: The Management of Law and Order in Eight Communities. Cambridge, Mass.: Harvard University Press, 1968.

__________, ed. The Metropolitan Enigma: Inquiries into the Nature and Dimensions of America's "Urban Crisis." Cambridge, Mass.: Harvard University Press, 1966.

__________, George L. Kelling. "Broken Windows." *Atlantic Monthly*, March 1982.

Wright, Louis B. The Atlantic Frontier: colonial American civilization, 1607-1763. NY: Alfred A. Knopf, 1947.

Zorbaugh, Harvey. The Gold Coast and the Slums. Chicago, Il: University of Chicago Press, 1929.

ABOUT THE AUTHOR

Eugene Alper has worked in code enforcement for more than twenty-five years, learning, thinking, teaching, and writing about it. Certified as a building, property maintenance, and zoning inspector, Eugene has Master's Degrees in Public Administration and Politics. He has taught code enforcement classes at annual conferences of the California Association of Code Enforcement, the American Association of Code Enforcement, and EduCode.

www.ingramcontent.com/pod-product-compliance
Lightning Source LLC
Chambersburg PA
CBHW060109260726
48658CB00004B/1471